PRESSING FORWARD

575 Shelton Road
Collierville, TN 38017
Tel: (901) 853-9827
www.colliervillechurchofchrist.com

Collierville Church of Christ
Simply Christians, Serving Christ

CHURCH OF
CHRIST

COLLIERVILLE

Trent Childers
Evangelist

tchilders@colliervillechurchofchrist.com
Cel: (731) 727-5652

PRESSING FORWARD

BIBLE-BASED ADDICTION RECOVERY

Trent Childers

ISBN-10: 1941972276
ISBN-13: 978-1941972274

Library of Congress Control Number: 2014954980

Published by Start2Finish Books
PO Box 680, Bowie, Texas 76230
www.start2finish.org

Printed in the United States of America

Unless otherwise noted, all Scripture quotations are from the *New King James Version*. Copyright © 1979, 1980, 1982 by Thomas Nelson, Inc. Used by permission. All rights reserved.

Cover Design: Josh Feit, Evangela.com

I dedicate this book to my mother, Sylvia Childers.

Thank you for waking me up when my head was in the clouds. Thank you for believing in me. It is refreshing to know I have my sweet mother as a fellow soldier of Jesus. I absolutely adore you and lovingly dedicate this book to you.

CONTENTS

FOREWORD

I was addicted to drugs and all the attendant sins for fifteen years, spent about seven years in and out of institutions, and spent five years in one stretch for kidnapping a police officer. I obeyed the gospel and spent another two and a half years in prison. I was released from prison in 1989 and established Project Rescue. I graduated from Memphis School of Preaching in 1993. My wife and I established an in-house recovery program in 2007. I have been ministering to addicts and alcoholics for 25 years.

In my opinion, the book you are about to read was written for such a time as this. Addiction is a sin problem and sin addiction (Gal. 6:1) and is the territory of the church. This is why we need more gospel preachers like Trent Childers writing material on this subject. Addiction is a spiritual sickness (Gal. 5:17), and the Bible is God's medicine (Psa. 119:11; Jas. 1:21) for the addict and alcoholic. Addiction imprisons the addict, and God's Word shows the way to freedom (John 8:31-32).

I penned this poem in prison:

> *Bricks and bars do not a prison make alone,*
> *A prison there is also stronger than steel and stone,*
> *created is this bind,*
> *by the working of our own spirit and mind,*

and the way out no one can find,
if they choose to remain blind.

With a higher power and the big book, Alcoholics Anonymous help men and women to live alcohol/drug-free lives. But the church of Christ, with the Highest Power and the Biggest Book, help men and women to live alcohol/drug-free lives and to enjoy eternal life in the life to come! The Project Rescue Addiction Recovery program enjoys a success rate (40%) that is double the best secular programs enjoy. The reason for this is that we are Bible-based and church-focused. For the same reasons, *Pressing Forward* is an excellent book.

In Christian concern,
Ronnie Crocker

Program Manager
Project Rescue Addiction Recovery

PREFACE

Think about the following two concepts:

1. Teaching someone the Bible.
2. Teaching someone addiction recovery.

Are these two concepts separate or are they related?

We live in a society in which teaching the Bible and aiding in addiction recovery are separated, but I submit to you that they go together. In fact, I emphatically declare it! This book argues that in order to obtain the best kind of change, one must incorporate the Bible into the recovery process. In truth, it should be the very foundation of healing.

I was a resident in an in-house rehabilitation program in 2004. It was a state facility, so they taught the Twelve Step model. I was taught (indeed, had already been taught in many Twelve Step meetings) that alcoholism was a disease, and I believed it. At the end of 2006, I obtained employment with a state drug-rehab facility where I taught the disease model to clients and their families. As a Bible believer, I attempted to reconcile the disease concept with God's Word, but it never seemed right. I finally left that facility in November 2008 and began work as a supported evangelist. Eventually, I realized that the Bible could not be reconciled with the disease model.

I had a desire to start Bible-based addiction recovery meetings and researched people who were already involved in such work. This goal was put on hold, however, as my wife and I decided to take part in the Memphis School of Preaching. I graduated from there in 2011 and obtained a B.S. in Ministry from Amridge University in December 2012. In the fall of 2012, I was talking with Torrey Clark, a fellow Memphis School of Preaching graduate and dear friend, about the need for Bible-based addiction recovery meetings. We discussed how these gatherings should be a place where people would be taught how to overcome struggles based upon the lessons of the Bible. Instead of being content with the discontinuation of harmful, addictive behavior, our goal was to convert people to Jesus Christ, teach them to faithfully serve Him, and thereby purify their souls. This goal in mind, we agreed, "Attendees will need a guide."

Thus, *Pressing Forward* was born.

Bruce Hatcher and Charles Harris, also dear friends, came "on board" to help with the effort. Over time, I noticed that many feel the need to incorporate a Twelve Step model into recovery meetings, but I was more interested in how people recovered from addiction in the first century. There was no disease model then. People were able to recover through the teachings of the gospel alone, using God's Word as their guide. People can discontinue an addictive behavior apart from the gospel; I am not saying that the Twelve Steps is ineffective. *Pressing Forward* is bigger than simply discontinuing a behavior, however. It is about healing in this life and in the next.

This book is not intended to be exhaustive, although it covers a lot of ground. Our goal is to be concise, prompting the reader to delve deeper into personal study and spiritual reflection. This book is divided into three main sections. The first defines and sets forth the effects of addiction, as well as the proposition that the Bible is key to correct thinking. We start with the understanding that the Bible is fully inspired of God, and therefore inerrant and authoritative. It is outside the scope of this work to delve into a study of the nature of biblical inspiration, but the evidence overwhelmingly shows the Bible is of divine origin; we encourage you to investigate the matter for yourself. The second section offers practical, biblical counsel and teaches how to become active in overcoming addiction. The third and final section provides Bible-based teaching on how best to follow Jesus faithfully.

We are not medical professionals, and this book is not intended to give, or be a substitute for, professional medical advice. It is, in no way, a substitute for medical detoxification. Withdrawal symptoms and behavior can be severe enough to risk a person's life, and we ask such readers to seek medical help first and foremost. If you have been abusing alcohol or other drugs, then please consult a physician. *Pressing Forward* is for those who have already undergone medical detoxification, if needed, and are fully on the path to recovery.

There is an Appendix at the end of the book that deals with the disease model, but is in no way an exhaustive study. There are already multiple, tome-like volumes written about that subject. Our intent is to provoke the reader toward further investigation. We ask that you weigh the evidence and realize that the Bible is a guide for healing the body, as well as the soul. Lastly, an additional Appendix contains a personal story of someone who has overcome addiction and is now serving Jesus. The story is meant to inspire hope and serve as a reminder that you are not alone in your struggle, and neither is it hopeless.

The "Cliff" sections are true, although "Cliff" is not the true name of the individual. The gentleman to whom these events happened, however, wrote them.

Trent Childers

INTRODUCTION

Cliff awoke in a motel room. He did not know where he was or how he got there. He looked around and saw some empty vodka bottles on the floor. Feeling very confused and frightened, he looked out the motel room window and saw his truck correctly parked. He sat down on the bed trying to remember how he had come to be there. He remembered drinking at a bar, but that was all until waking up here.

Another bottle of vodka lay on the bed. Cliff picked it up ready to take another drink, but stopped. He said to himself, "I have to stop drinking; I can't continue like this." It was not the first time Cliff had awoken in a strange place, unaware of how he had arrived. As he held the bottle in his hands, debating on whether to take a drink or not, he noticed a Bible on the nightstand by the bed. He put the bottle down and started reading the Bible. His mind was so hazy from drinking that he could not understand the blurring words. Bursting into tears, he knew he had to stop drinking. He was tired of the misery, pain, and loneliness; he was desperate for something different. He put the Bible back on the nightstand, picked up the bottle of vodka, and took another drink. Confused, frightened and crying, Cliff desired something better but had no idea where to turn. Was it possible to escape from this kind of despair? If so, what was the key to change?

* * *

We submit to you that it is God; He is the key to change.

When we say God, we do not refer to some vague "Higher Power," which people understand as they wish, but rather to the God of the Bible. Think about this: We are created beings. As such, we are subject to our Creator. Think about the arrogance and absurdity of not giving Him the glory of this life, when without Him we would not even exist. If our Creator has communicated to us, informing us of how He desires us to live, then logic and reason demand that we adhere to that message. The Holy Bible—divine in origin—is God's Word to His children.

Is it possible to overcome addiction without the Bible? Sure it is. Many people who have recovered from addictive behaviors do not credit the Bible as their inspiration, motivation, or guide. For example, Robert Downey, Jr. credits his recovery to family, therapy, meditation, twelve-step recovery programs, yoga and the practice of Wing Chun Jung Kung Fu.

The Bible, however, is not just about overcoming addiction. Contemplate these words of Jesus: "And do not fear those who kill the body but cannot kill the soul. But rather fear Him who is able to destroy both soul and body in hell" (Matt. 10:28). It would be a tragedy indeed, to escape the hell of our own making to spend an eternity in the hell not created by or for us. We are concerned with addiction recovery, but more so with eternal salvation, of which Jesus is the author (Heb. 5:9). Understanding that there is a Creator who has revealed His will, why would you want to take any other option?

Let us return to the concept of "change." We do not refer merely to putting aside the behavior with which you are struggling, even though that is a necessary step on the path to recovery. An addictive behavior such as gambling, drinking, viewing pornography, excessive spending illicit sex, lying, gossip, to name a few, is only a symptom of a broader, false view. When we say change, we refer to an inside out change, which not only includes discontinuing the addictive behavior, but also changing the way you view the world and being led to heaven. Accordingly, a liar who becomes frequently intoxicated can put down the bottle and still be a liar. He may no longer "hit the bottle," but that does not mean he is headed in the right direction. This book puts forth the proposition that you must have the map that leads to the correct destination. Stephen R. Covey wrote:

> Suppose you wanted to arrive at a specific location in central Chicago. ... But suppose you were given the wrong map. ... Can you imagine the frustration, the ineffectiveness of trying to reach your destination? You might try to work on your *behavior*—you could try harder, be more diligent, double your speed. But your efforts would only succeed in getting you to the wrong place faster. You might work on your *attitude*—you could think more positively... The point is, you'd still be lost. The fundamental problem has nothing to do with your behavior or your attitude. It has everything to do with having a wrong map.[1]

The correct map for life is the Bible.

The Apostle Paul said, "I press toward the goal for the prize of the upward call of God in Christ Jesus" (Phil. 3:14). You may at this moment find it hard to believe that you can actually press forward after the lifestyle you have led, but we assure you that you can. We do not assure you that you will, for that is up to you, but you can.

Will the change come overnight? No.

Will it be difficult? Yes.

Will it take great effort on your part? Yes.

Will you have to confront fears? Yes.

Will it be worth it? Absolutely.

This book does not promise "a walk in the park" here on earth. How could it, when God never did? However, He did promise through

---

1. Stephen R. Covey, *The 7 Habits of Highly Effective People* (New York: Free Press, 1989, 2004), 23, 24.

Jesus Christ that we could find joy and contentment in this life, as well as eternal life with Him. That is what this is about—joy and eternal life through Jesus Christ.

PART ONE: THE CONCEPT

It is the science behind addiction, with consideration towards the successful methods of recovery employed in recent decades, that the following concepts are submitted. We seek to offer the reader the best method of recovery available, one that results in the best resulting quality of life. This is the concept.

1

THE SCIENCE OF ADDICTION

In light of recent discoveries about the brain, previous definitions of addiction are being refined. Not long ago, the prevailing thought on the subject was exemplified by the following statement: "Research has shown the brain's reward circuitry is modified in addicts, making them crave 'rewards,' such as alcohol and other drugs... Addiction is a chronic brain disorder and not simply a behavior problem."

New studies, however, suggest that while the observation of modified brain circuitry was valid, the resulting conclusion was incorrect. The term *neuroplasticity* (also called brain plasticity) describes "the brain's ability to reorganize itself by forming new neural connections throughout life. Neuroplasticity allows the neurons (nerve cells) in the brain to compensate for injury and disease and to adjust their activities in response to new situations or to changes in their environment."

Paul Bach-y-Rita, a neuroscientist also known as the "father of brain plasticity," explained plasticity with this example:

> If you are driving from here to Milwaukee and the main bridge goes out, first you are paralyzed. Then you take old secondary roads through the farmland. Then you use these roads more; you find shorter paths to use to get where you want to go, and you start to get there faster. These "secondary" neural pathways are "unmasked" or exposed

and strengthened as they are used. The "unmasking" process is generally thought to be one of the principal ways in which the plastic brain reorganizes itself.[1]

The brain is complex and amazing, just as addiction is controlling and dangerous. *Psychology Today* states:

> Addiction is a condition that results when a person ingests a substance (alcohol, cocaine, nicotine) or engages in an activity (gambling) that can be pleasurable but the continued use of which becomes compulsive and interferes with ordinary life responsibilities, such as work or relationships, or health.[2]

SUBSTANCE ABUSE

It is doubtful that anyone thinks about what drugs will do to their body before using them. Addicts seek immediate gratification or the "high." What is it that actually occurs in the body as a result of drug use? In an interview with Dr. Brad Harrub, who holds a Ph.D. in human anatomy and neurobiology and was listed in *Who's Who Among Scientists and Researchers*, answered some questions regarding the physiological effects brought on by drugs. What follows are the questions we asked Dr. Harrub and his professional responses.

Q: What are the immediate physiological effects of using alcohol, stimulants, barbiturates, opiates, etc.?

A: The nervous system is controlled by neurotransmitters. Under normal circumstances, the brain regulates the release and re-uptake of these neurochemicals. Drugs artificially alter the amount of neurotransmitters in the brain, either increasing or decreasing the

---

1. Norman Doidge, *The Brain That Changes Itself* (New York: Viking; 2007).

2. http://www.psychologytoday.com/basics/addiction

amount of neurochemicals. For instance, high levels of dopamine in an area of the brain called the "nucleus accumbens" results in a feeling of pleasure. Drugs that are often stimulants, such as cocaine or nicotine, block the re-uptake of dopamine, thus resulting in elevated levels, which lead to a feeling of pleasure. Opiates, such as heroin and oxycodone, depress nerve transmission specifically in the sensory pain pathway of the brain and spinal cord; that's why these drugs are effective at depressing pain. Drugs such as these alter the normal amount of neurotransmitters as soon as the body detects them.

Q: Explain the process the brain and body go through when regressing from sobriety to intoxication.

A: Most people are familiar with using rubbing alcohol to kill bacteria around a cut. We do this because alcohol breaks down proteins, lipids, the bacteria and, in some cases, viruses. The same thing happens in the human body. At high enough levels, alcohol damages cells, specifically in the liver, the "filter" of the body, which is why alcoholics often develop cirrhosis. When alcohol is consumed, it is the liver's job to break it down and remove it from the system. However, alcohol can readily cross the cell membrane of any cell; this can happen as soon as it reaches the stomach. Once in the bloodstream, alcohol can journey toward the brain and spinal cord; when it crosses over the blood/brain barrier, it begins affecting the central nervous system. The central nervous system (CNS) is normally dependent on your five senses to analyze your environment and elicit appropriate responses. Alcohol interferes with the CNS's ability to analyze everything properly, thus people begin to experience a delay or trouble with sensory organs, speech, and sweat glands. Thus, individuals who drink will find themselves exhibiting the typical symptoms of slurred speech, disturbed balance, blurred vision, dulling of pain, etc. Because it has the ability to cross cell membranes quickly, alcohol can also affect the outer layer of the brain—known as the frontal cortex—the region commonly associated with inhibitions and conscious thought. Additionally, if alcohol is drunk in abundance, then the liver becomes unable to break it down quickly enough, allowing it to circulate throughout the body causing damage to other cells and putting more alcohol into the CNS.

Q: What physiological effects occur after the "high" has worn off?

A: When a "high" wears off, the drugs that were stimulating the pleasure center of the brain are "reuptaken" back into nerve cells and the pleasure center is no longer stimulated. The difference in amounts of these neurochemicals released, such as when, for instance, a methamphetamine is introduced to the human body, would be like going from a backyard kiddie pool with small amounts of dopamine being released occasionally to help maintain your mood, to suddenly being thrown into the ocean. Many addictive behaviors and substances cause nerves to "fire," which produces increased levels of chemicals, like dopamine. Other drugs, such as cocaine, don't clean up after "firing." Normally neurons will reuptake the neurochemcials not used/needed once the signal has been sent to other neurons. Cocaine, however, does not allow the cell to reuptake the dopamine that was released, which then makes this excitatory neurochemical available for surrounding neurons. This in turn causes more neuronal firing, but also sets a new "high water mark" for these neurochemicals to achieve pleasure.

Q: Explain the craving process that takes place in the brain.

A: These physiological changes are just the beginning. New high levels placed on the pleasure pathway cause the neurons to seek repetition of this event. It's at this point that the drug of choice becomes viewed as a survival tool rather than as an escape or temporary pleasure. Priorities and behaviors change as the addict seeks more and more ways to satisfy his or her new desire. As the addict continues to increase dopamine levels through drug-related behavior, the brain responds by reducing normal dopamine production. Eventually, this cycle causes massive problems as the decrease in normal dopamine production causes a cascade of changes throughout the brain. Recent research has also demonstrated that nerves will increase or decrease the number of receptors for specific neurochemicals after prolonged abuse.

Q: What starts to happen physiologically after long term repeated use of a substance?

A: The brain is supposed to regulate the amount of neurotransmitters released. If drugs are taken habitually, then the brain no longer functions properly—and the effects can be devastating. The feedback mechanism that normally regulates everything begins working improperly. Not only can it be detrimental to the brain, but the brain, as the control center of the body, can also negatively affect other areas of the body.

PORNOGRAPHY

Addiction to pornography is an "elephant in the room," so to speak. There is a strong social stigma attached to what is labeled as sexually deviant behavior, which seems to make it more difficult for people to confess an addiction to it. Like alcohol and other drugs, however, the same process occurs in the brain with avid pornography users. Therefore, pornography is as much a drug as methamphetamine, cocaine, and alcohol. When describing porn's effect to a U.S. Senate committee, Dr. Jeffrey Satinover of Princeton University said, "It is as though we have devised a form of heroin 100 times more powerful than before, usable in the privacy of one's own home and injected directly to the brain through the eyes."

In light of Dr. Satinover's claim, we sought expertise from someone in the field of counseling who has dealt with patients addicted to pornography. Dr. Jerry L. Martin received his Ph.D. in Marriage and Family Therapy and has since become a licensed family counselor, member of The American Association of Christian Counselors, a professional member of The American Counseling Association, and an associate member of The American Association of Marriage and Family Therapists. We asked Dr. Martin questions related to pornography and its effects on the human brain and body. What follows are our questions and his professional responses.

Q: What is the definition pornography?

A: A typical definition of pornography would identify sexually explicit images, writing, or other material whose primary purpose is to cause sexual excitement or arousal. Pornography addiction, like all other addictions, is a compulsive and repeated behavior that is performed regardless of the negative consequences. The real addiction is to lust, however, not pornography itself. The behavior is an attempt to satisfy emotional needs and sexual gratification through viewing or visualizing pornography. Masturbation is the usual means of stimulating climax.

Q: What are the effects of pornography to the viewer?

A: Physiological: prolonged exposure to pornography, particularly cyber-pornography, can cause irritability, restlessness, sleeplessness, distress, anxiety, depression, headaches, dizziness, and even body aches. In spite of the negative effects, the user will typically crave more of the behavior, yet begin to have an increasing physiological tolerance to the exposure. Our internal chemistry produces addictive chemicals and stimulated highs are produced by the release of internal brain chemicals. Prolonged use causes the resulting excitement to feel normal and, thus, the body demands an increased use of the substance. Spiritually: pornography, like other stimuli of lust, robs us of a pure and intimate relationship with God, while perverting and diminishing intimacy intended to be enjoyed in God-ordained relationships. God cannot be blamed for the urges, actions, behaviors, or their associated consequences. The inspired writer James describes the progressive nature of lust and provides an appropriate explanation of the effects pornography has on a person spiritually: "Let no one say when he is tempted, 'I am tempted by God'; for God cannot be tempted by evil, nor does He Himself tempt anyone. But each one is tempted when he is drawn away by his own desires and enticed. Then, when desire has conceived, it gives birth to sin; and sin, when it is full-grown, brings forth death" (Jas. 1:13-15).

The Bible makes it clear that whatever we allow into our minds can have an influence upon our lives. What is hidden in the heart determines what and who we become (Matt. 15:18-19; Mark 7:20-23). In the book of Job, there is a description of behavior applicable to those involved in pornography:

> Others have been with those who rebel against the light; they do not want to know its ways, nor abide in its paths. The murderer arises at dawn; he kills the poor and the needy, and at night he is as a thief. And the eye of the adulterer waits for the twilight, saying, "No eye will see me." And he disguises his face. In the dark they dig into houses, they shut themselves up by day; they do not know the light. For the morning is the same to him as thick darkness, for he is familiar with the terrors of thick darkness.
>
> Job 24:13-17

According to this passage, what begins with a deceitful secret breeds lust and ultimately leads to bondage (Tit. 3:3; Eph. 2:1-3). The thought/behavior cycle of our minds is a complex, progressive battle between our psychological/physiological and rational/spiritual selves. First, there comes the stimulus (images, sounds, smell, memory), followed then by associative emotions and thoughts (excitement, curiosity, wonder). Our body responds to these reactions with a chemical release and bodily response (increased heart rate, dilated eyes, tight muscles). Then our brain kicks in, giving us second thoughts (*I really shouldn't, but it would feel so good*), doubt or justification (*Will it ever go away? I can't help it, why try?*) and, finally, our response (most likely giving in). In the end, we are left with reflection (*What have I done?*) and a new set of feelings and thoughts associated with guilt and shame. For an addict, this cycle is never ending.

REACTION OF THE BRAIN

Whether one ingests a drug, views pornographic images, or compulsively gambles, the brain reacts in the same basic manner. Pleasure-causing chemicals (e.g. serotonin, dopamine, endorphins) are released from the "reward pathways" in the brain. These pleasure centers of the brain chemically respond to things such as food, sex, and social interactions, providing a mood associated with these specific actions. These chemical responses serve as a reward system that can give motivation and incentive: "In simplistic terms, activation of the pathway tells the individual to repeat what it just did to get that reward."

CONCLUSION

Addiction can take on many forms; we can even damage our brains without ingesting substances. Gambling, overeating, gossiping, lying, impulse spending, etc. can all ruin our lives. Understanding the physical, psychological, social, and spiritual effects of addiction should provide the addict with the motivation to discontinue his/her current lifestyle and Press Forward in living according to the guidelines prescribed by the Great Physician.

PRESSING POINT:

*You do not have to remain a slave to your addiction.
The cycle of addiction can and must be broken.*

2

THE BIBLE & ADDICTION

Not only does the Bible address addiction, it defines it quite clearly. In the context of fornication, Paul wrote, "I will not be brought under the power of any" (1 Cor. 6:12). The Greek word *exousiasthesomai* is translated by Thayer as, "to have power or authority, use power ... to be master of any one, exercise authority over one."[1] Addiction is allowing something to exercise authority over you; the addict submits himself to the master of addiction and allows the practice to consume him.

Jesus defined addiction more simply: "Most assuredly, I say to you, whoever commits sin is a slave of sin. And a slave does not abide in the house forever, but a son abides forever. Therefore if the Son makes you free, you shall be free indeed" (John 8:34-36). The verb "commit" is used here to express continuous action, thereby suggesting that whoever continues in sin also continues to be a slave to it. Jesus was speaking of contemporary, stubborn people who rejected His deity and were entangled in their own selfish desires. Addicts are slaves to sin. Sin, according to Paul, reigns in one's body, demanding obedience (Rom. 6:12). It wants us to serve it, but Paul beseeches us to present ourselves "as instruments of righteousness to God" (6:13) so that we might be set free from sin's mastery over us (6:18).

---

1. Joseph Henry Thayer, *A Greek-English Lexicon of the New Testament*, 4th ed. (Grand Rapids: Baker, 1977), 225-26.

THE BIBLE & SEXUAL ADDICTION

Solomon vividly portrays sexual addiction in Prov. 6:26, "For by means of a harlot a man is reduced to a crust of bread; and an adulteress will prey upon his precious life." Here the man is taken to the poor house because of excess spending on a prostitute. He begins his lustful pleasures with a prostitute, but eventually turns to another man's wife, an adulteress. The addiction consumes his life; it becomes his master.

Peter wrote about those with a sexual addiction, describing them as having,

> Eyes full of adultery and that cannot cease from sin, enticing unstable souls. They have a heart trained in covetous practices, and are accursed children. They have forsaken the right way and gone astray. ... While they promise them liberty, they themselves are slaves of corruption; for by whom a person is overcome, by him also he is brought into bondage.
>
> 2 Pet. 2:14-15, 19

These people are consumed by sexual perversions (cf. Matt. 5:28). They cannot stop their sinful behavior because they have allowed God's Word to be too far removed from them, and while it is kept from their hearts, they will continue in sin (cf. Psa. 119:11). Their hearts are "trained in covetous practices;" it has become longstanding practice, and as a result, they are "accursed." They are headed down the wrong path. Ironically, they profess liberty, but they are "slaves of corruption," Peter explains, "for by whom a person is overcome, by him he is brought into bondage" (2 Pet. 2:19). We are not truly happy in the relationship, only superficially so; addiction, quite simply, is a mass of chains binding us to a false, deceitful master.

THE BIBLE & ALCOHOL

Solomon addresses the woes of alcohol, affirming, "Wine is a mocker, Strong drink is a brawler, And whoever is led astray by it is not wise" (Prov. 20:1). These are not his only words on the matter, however. In Prov. 23, he once again, and rather glaringly, describes alcohol addiction in vivid terms:

> Who has woe? Who has sorrow? Who has contentions? Who has complaints? Who has wounds without cause? Who has redness of eyes? Those who linger long at the wine, Those who go in search of mixed wine. Do not look on the wine when it is red, When it sparkles in the cup, When it swirls around smoothly; At the last it bites like a serpent, And stings like a viper. Your eyes will see strange things, And your heart will utter perverse things. Yes, you will be like one who lies down in the midst of the sea, Or like one who lies at the top of the mast, saying: "They have struck me, but I was not hurt; They have beaten me, but I did not feel it. When shall I awake, that I may seek another drink?
>
> Prov. 23:29-35

The addict Solomon describes subjected himself to immorality and punishment because his judgment and reasoning were hindered by alcohol. Study those last two lines closely. The addict is beaten, but he "did not feel it," as the alcohol numbed him, then immediately wonders when he would wake up so he could have another drink. Despite the harmful consequences of his inebriated misadventures, the addiction has consumed him so fully that he wants another drink, despite knowing it is the reason for his suffering.

THE BIBLE & DRUGS

Addiction to drugs other than alcohol is also included in the Scriptures. Notice the "works of the flesh" as listed by Paul (Gal. 5:19-21). First, the word "sorcery" is included in the list, and it includes drug use, which a definition of the Greek word and an historical study will show. Second, after listing "works of the flesh," Paul uses the phrase, "and the like" (Gal. 5:19-21) which would include the use of other mind altering drugs. This does not include their legitimate medicinal use (cf. 1 Tim. 5:23). Third, within the very word "drunkenness" is a definition of "intoxication," which is certainly not limited to alcohol.

The Bible addresses the valleys of addiction, but it also offers the solution to suffering under a false master. It is the goal of this book to expose these answers and provide a guide that can lead the addict away from temptation and back into the loving embrace of the true Master.

PRESSING POINT:

Not only is the problem of addiction mentioned in the Bible, but the solution to the problem is stated as well.

3

CHANGE YOUR THINKING

D o you recall the short story about Cliff in the *Introduction*? We left
him at a turning point in his life, the moment when he realized that
he no longer wanted to live enslaved to the bottle. The first time Cliff got
drunk, however, he enjoyed it. It started as a weekend thing, just a few
beers with friends. Then it was a drink or two after work to help him relax.
Eventually, it was an everyday ritual.

No matter how often Cliff drank, he never stopped until he was
completely drunk. The more Cliff drank, however, the worse he felt, and
the more ashamed he was of the resulting actions. It wasn't fun anymore.
He no longer felt the lightness and ease that alcohol used to bring. So he
started trying other drugs to achieve some sort of peace or happiness, but
he never found it. Everything revolved around alcohol for Cliff. He told
himself he wasn't going to drink as much or that he would wait until later
in the day, but as soon as Cliff took that first sip, all his inhibitions were
gone. When he would finally come to after an afternoon of binging, he
felt confused and angry, so angry. Sometimes he started drinking again to
make it easier. What other option was there?

* * *

A saying often used in regard to computers can also be used to describe how our minds work: "Garbage in, garbage out." More simply, when you put something into your mind, it will come back out in one form or another. Jesus understood this concept long before computers. In a response to the Pharisees and scribes, he exclaimed, "What comes out of a man, that defiles a man. For from within, out of the heart of men, proceed evil thoughts, adulteries, fornications, murders, thefts, covetousness, wickedness, deceit, lewdness, an evil eye, blasphemy, pride, foolishness. All these evil things come from within and defile a man" (Mark 7:20-23).

In these lines, "heart" refers to the mind, and these "evil things" of which Jesus spoke "come from within." Outward actions cannot change unless there is first an inward cleansing. After years of indulging in addictive behaviors, the mind becomes warped, rewired as it were, and needs to be trained to think in a different, healthier manner. The mind needs to be washed free of its evils, and then it can begin to heal.

How should you begin to cleanse your mind of addiction? First, focus on the long-term consequences of what you are doing. Think back to Cliff's example in the beginning of this chapter. All he thought about was the immediate result; he drank and became happier, more relaxed, and even numb. Did he ever think about how it would affect his family or job? He failed to think about the long-term effects and focused only on immediate satisfaction, or short-term benefits; this is a fundamental thinking flaw. As long as an addict persists in such thinking, s/he will not be able to overcome his/her self-destructive behavior.

Why not indulge in some fun? Why not take care of this craving and just be done with it? Family, friends, health—all of these should motivate an addict not to abuse substances, but what is the ultimate goal s/he should focus on to avoid being "brought under the power of any"? It is in the word's of Paul that we find a clear answer to this question:

- "I press toward the goal for the prize of the upward call of God in Christ Jesus" (Phil. 3:14).

- "But I discipline my body and bring it into subjection, lest, when I have preached to others, I myself should become disqualified" (1 Cor. 9:27).

- "For to me, to live is Christ, and to die is gain" (Phil. 1:21).

- "I have fought the good fight, I have finished the race, I have kept the faith. Finally, there is laid up for me the crown of righteousness" (2 Tim. 4:7-8).

Paul looked "for the prize." He disciplined his body so that he would not "become disqualified." Christ was his life; thus, death would be his ending glory. He "fought the good fight," because he had his mind on "the crown of righteousness." Are you willing to overcome the craving for immediate gratification in exchange for the crown?

When we finally allow ourselves to see the final goal, we must then welcome God's Word to dwell within us. Actually, this is the key to focusing on long-term thinking. The Word of God is powerful (Heb. 4:12)! However, it must be studied before it can be accessed.

I remember a poster in my high school science classroom that said something like "Learning by Osmosis," and had Garfield sitting down with a stack of books on his head. Obviously, we have to do more than this; we must make the active decision to put forth the effort for God's Word to inhabit us. The psalmist penned, "Your word I have hidden in my heart, That I might not sin against You" (Psa. 119:11). What is the greatest weapon against sin? "Your word." Fill your mind with that which is pure, as Paul admonished: "Finally, brethren, whatever things are true, whatever things are noble, whatever things are just, whatever things are pure, whatever things are lovely, whatever things are of good report, if there is any virtue and if there is anything praiseworthy—meditate on these things" (Phil. 4:8).

For God's Word to take up residence within us, we must meditate upon it. The gospel changes lives if we allow it (Rom. 1:16; cf. 1 Cor. 6:9-

11). Studying God's Word and seeking to apply it honestly will result in a purer, healthier life.

Finally, spend time with other faithful servants of Christ. According to Acts 2:42-47, the Jerusalem church is not merely a collection of believers who gather for worship and then disperse. It is a family, tied together through faith and focused on the glory of God. "So continuing daily with one accord in the temple, and breaking bread from house to house, they ate their food with gladness and simplicity of heart, praising God and having favor with all the people" (Act 2:46-47; cf. Eph. 2:19; 3:14-21, and notice the usage of the word "brethren" in the New Testament to describe Christians). Your fellow Christians will build you up, contribute to your pure thinking, and take your hand if you stumble.

Dealing with your past and addressing your inner emotions (addressed further in Part 3) will help you change your thinking. Moreover, study the Bible, for in its pages are the answers to our despair, emptiness, and the very salvation of our souls.

PRESSING POINT:

When facing temptation to use, think about the consequences, study your Bible, and spend time with Christians.

4

CHANGE YOUR BEHAVIOR

Cliff wanted to stop drinking, but how could he? Someone introduced him to the idea that he could choose to stop drinking if he wanted to—that it was up to him. At first, it seemed impossible, but he decided to try not drinking, and it worked. For a while. Every day, Cliff would wake up and tell himself that he did not have to drink. He realized it was possible not to drink, but he never attempted to change his lifestyle. Eventually, he made the choice to drink again, and the cycle started over. Until Cliff chose to change how he lived, he would never be able to give up his dependence on alcohol.

* * *

It is possible to overcome a sinful lifestyle seemingly consumed by addictive behavior. However, it is first crucial to understand sin and to take it seriously. So what is sin? Simply stated by John, "Whoever commits sin also commits lawlessness, and sin is lawlessness" (1 John 3:4). Sin involves breaking God's law, and doing such is not a matter to be taken lightly, as it carries a penalty of death (Rom. 6:23), and it costs Jesus Christ his blood (Matt. 26:28; Phil. 2:5-8; Heb. 12:2).

Sin is lawlessness and the flouting of God's Word, this is made clear by John. But what is the process of sin? "But each one is tempted when he is drawn away by his own desires and enticed. Then, when desire has conceived, it gives birth to sin; and sin, when it is full-grown, brings forth death. Do not be deceived, my beloved brethren" (Jas. 1:14-16).

First, you have a desire or want. There is no sin in desire itself; you do nothing wrong in wanting, and you have the ability to walk away without shame. It is only after "desire has conceived" that sin is born and then "brings forth death." In contemplating sin, however, remember that you are the decision maker; you alone will choose to sin and are accountable for the repercussions that follow. A more important question to ask is whether or not someone who has fallen deeply into the muck and mire of sin can still climb back out? Is it too late for them? Carefully read Paul's words to the Corinthians:

> Do you not know that the unrighteous will not inherit the kingdom of God? Do not be deceived. Neither fornicators, nor idolaters, nor adulterers, nor homosexuals, nor sodomites, nor thieves, nor covetous, nor drunkards, nor revilers, nor extortioners will inherit the kingdom of God. And such were some of you. But you were washed, but you were sanctified, but you were justified in the name of the Lord Jesus and by the Spirit of our God.
>
>   1 Cor. 6:9-11

Paul presents quite the list of sins in this passage. Are you struggling with one or more of these? If so, know that you are neither alone nor forsaken. These people to whom Paul was speaking had participated in illicit sex (sex outside of marriage), covetousness, homosexuality, thievery, drunkenness, and more, but something happened to cause Paul to say, "such were some of *you*" (emphasis added). These people were given a fresh start through the gospel. They became "new creations" (2 Cor. 5:17), their sins washed away. Does this mean their desires were completely erased or that they would never again have an issue with craving to participate in such activities? No, but they were given a reason to press forward with the hope and assurance that their past sins had been forgiven, and that they were now walking in the light (1 John 1:7-9). In allowing Christ to forgive them, they committed themselves to a life of service to Him.

There were people present on the day of Pentecost who had participated in the murder of Jesus (Acts 2:36), only to see him resurrected (2:32). They were cut to the heart after hearing this message and wanted to change their lives. Peter did not then tell them that they had no hope of atonement. There is always hope. On the contrary, he told them what to do in order to have hope of eternal life: "Repent, and let every one of you be baptized in the name of Jesus Christ for the remission of sins; and you shall receive the gift of the Holy Spirit. For the promise is to you and to your children, and to all who are afar off, as many as the Lord our God will call" (Acts 2:38-29).

Before Paul was blessed with the vision of Christ resurrected, he had dedicated his life to destroying Christianity. Paul described himself as "a blasphemer, a persecutor, and an insolent man," but these transgressions were forgiven because they were done "ignorantly in unbelief" (1 Tim. 1:13). How can a man go from committing these horrible acts to being a faithful missionary of Christ? Paul realized that mercy and grace had been lavished upon him (1:13-14), which motivated him to serve Christ and forsake his old ways (Gal. 2:20).

Paul is a pattern for us to follow. He once sought to destroy Christianity but was eventually shown a different path and became a soldier of the cross. If he can commit to so drastic a change, then you can also change from the course you are currently traveling. Can you honestly look at Paul's transformation and say you have no hope? True hope for true change, as well as eternal benefits, resides only in Jesus Christ.

PRESSING POINT:

For your life to be different, you must change the way you live.
Change is difficult; however, in Jesus it is possible.

5

A BETTER LIFE

Cliff's life changed drastically after he went sober. He stopped drinking, yes, but then he tried to improve himself, which did not make his choice of abstinence any easier. Cliff had been introduced to some principles found in the Bible and had been trying, to the best of his ability, to apply those principles to his own life. And it was working. He no longer looked over his shoulder, wondering when the urge would rise. Now he could look people in the eye when speaking to them. He could look himself in the eye. Cliff was no longer disgusted at what he saw in the mirror. There were even times while driving that he would see a police car in his rear view mirror and not get nervous. Then, Cliff met a woman whom he would marry. Once he lived with the mindset that everything was about him, his needs, and his cravings. Now, however, he was thinking about the needs of others.

* * *

Jesus affirmed, "The thief does not come except to steal, and to kill, and to destroy. I have come that they may have life, and that they may have it more abundantly" (John 10:10). These words were addressed to those Jews who rejected who Christ was. They were rejecting the offer of an abundant life. Here, the word "abundantly" has several definitions:

- An excessive number, measure, rank, or need
- More than is necessary
- Abundantly, supremely
- Something further, more plainly
- Superior, extraordinary, surpassing, uncommon
- Pre-eminence, superiority, advantage, more remarkable, more excellent

The life Jesus offers is unsurpassed by any other. It is definitely true that Jesus offers hope of eternal life in heaven, but it is important to remember that joy in Jesus brings abundant life to us in the here and now.

There seems to be a notion in today's society that the sinful lifestyle is the happiest lifestyle on earth. After all, how can a life of deprivation and self-sacrifice be happy? A faithful, Christian life is a restrained one, without the great pleasures of life, so what happiness is there? Right? Paul, however, never thought this because he learned to be content in whatever state he found himself; he had true joy in Christ (Phil. 4:11-13). Even though a Christian must be willing to endure suffering for Christ (Matt. 5:10-12; 2 Tim. 3:12; 1 Pet. 4:15-16), the Christian life is better than any other. Mankind's greatest flaw is in thinking that the greatest pleasures in life are attained through possessions. They are not. The Christian life is the best there is because we can live with the hope of eternal salvation and the assurance that no one can rob us of it.

There is a great contrast between living the enslaved life of addiction and being led by the gospel of Christ. Notice the following chart:

Life of Addiction	Abundant Life in Christ
No hope of eternal life	Hope of eternal life
Dependence on substances/ behaviors for temporary contentment	Dependence upon Christ and happiness, despite external circumstances
Guilt prompted by behaviors	Forgiveness in Christ

Life of Addiction	Abundant Life in Christ
Hiding behaviors; paranoia of being caught	Freedom in Christ
Impaired physical and mental health	Healthy in body, mind, and soul
Negative influence on family and friends	Shining light for family and friends

This is not to say that a Christian will not suffer persecution. In fact, the faithful servant often does (2 Tim. 3:10-17; Matt. 5:10-12). Moreover, a Christian is not immune to disease or misfortune, but if we live a faithful, Christian life, we will have freedom in Christ. We will not have to be plagued with a lifetime of guilt and can influence others towards good. Being a faithful Christian will not save us from family division either; Christ taught of the necessity of loving Him more than family, despite how hard that may sometimes be (Matt. 10:34-42). However, a life committed to Christ is one that will experience true, lasting contentment, even in the midst of suffering.

Transitioning from the bondage of addiction to living in Christ is a process that takes genuine effort. A life subjected to addiction incurs a great deal of damage, both physically and mentally, not to mention the negative effect substance abuse can have on the relationships in one's life. Thus, an addict will have to learn to face the horrors of the past in order to take steps towards a better future. Thinking must be transformed and conformed to Christ (Rom. 12:1-2). Although facing the past and confronting fears is daunting, it is a process that will be well worth the effort. The beauty of Christianity is that you have a promised, continual cleansing of Christ's blood; the only condition is to continue walking in the light (1 John 1:5-10).

It is crucial that you do not set unrealistic expectations for yourself. Imagine walking into a kitchen and launching eggs everywhere; then you rip open a bag of coffee and shake it generously throughout the kitchen.

It does not matter why you did, only that you did. Realizing the damage you have done, you admit to being the perpetrator and apologize. Does the mess just disappear? Does your confession clean up the chaos? The harmful decisions of your past carry negative consequences; they will not simply disappear because of your decision to change. However, making the decision to change is crucial because it will determine where you live in eternity.

It is no accident that people who live this abundant life are not in and out of jail, fired from jobs for irresponsibility, or referred to as "the wrong sort of people." It is also no accident that people living with the plague of addiction experience these very same difficulties. Can you imagine a life in which you do not have to go to bed guilt-stricken, in which you do not have to create lies to conceal your addictive behavior, in which you do not continually let down those you love, in which you can have a blessed assurance of eternal life no matter what? Believe *that* you can have it. Believe because you *can* have it.

PRESSING POINT:

Do not settle for a miserable existence.
Jesus has a better life waiting for you.

6

TRUE CONTENTMENT

A few years have passed since Cliff drank or used drugs. He is married now, with a baby on the way. Life was far better than it once was. He no longer constantly thought about his next drink; that was not a problem anymore. It was rare when he even thought about drinking and when he did, the pressure was gone. Instead, he moved on to think about other things. He had learned biblical principles from people who were, at one time or another, trapped in the same hopeless state of mind he once was. However, Cliff still felt like he was missing something. He began to study his Bible on a daily basis, opening it to some random page and reading it for a while. There were parts he had trouble understanding and wanted to learn more about the Bible, where it came from, what it all meant. He attended various churches, but always left without any answers to his questions. He had even thought about trying other religions like Buddhism, but these never filled the emptiness.

Cliff's parents were members of the church of Christ, so he decided to visit the local congregation. They were offering a class designed to teach people how to instruct others in the Bible. Cliff thought that if he attended the class, then maybe his questions would be answered. It was not long until he realized just how lost in sin he was. It was great that he had become sober and was trying to live a better life, but according to the Bible, he was lost. After much study, Cliff learned about the death, burial, and resurrection of Jesus. More importantly, he learned how everyone should respond to it. As a result, he was baptized into Christ for the forgiveness of his sins. For the first time in his life, he had finally found what he was missing. Not only was his life better from sobriety and self-improvement, Cliff finally knew that when this temporary life ended, he would be ready for the eternal one to begin.

* * *

If you could ask someone about true contentment, whom would you ask? Would you go to the nearest prison and ask an inmate? I assume you answered no, because neither would I. Nevertheless, the person who wrote some of the most powerful statements regarding contentment did so from prison; he was a prisoner because he did what was right. Imagine being charged with a crime for doing the right thing. If there was ever a time to complain about mistreatment and not being content, that would be it. Yet Paul wrote the epistles to the Philippians as a prisoner, letters renowned for their joyous nature. The contrariness of this makes sense, however, when pondering Paul's outstanding character.

While in Philippi, Paul and Silas were arrested for helping someone (Acts 16:16-24). They were beaten "with rods. And when ... many stripes" had been inflicted upon them, they were cast into prison. And what did they do in prison? They prayed. "But at midnight Paul and Silas were praying and singing hymns to God, and the prisoners were listening to them" (Acts 16:22-25). Yes, they sang praises to God and prayed to Him. Even in the darkness of injustice and ignorance, they sought out the loving embrace of the Lord. This passage is reminiscent of the apostles' attitude in Acts 5:40-42 when they, too, were punished for "teaching and preaching Jesus as the Christ." While imprisoned, Paul and Silas even converted the jailer and his household (16:26-34)! What if they had complained to the jailer about the injustice of the situation? What if they had shared only bitterness and anger? Would the jailer have converted to Christ?

Later, Paul wrote one of the most staggering statements regarding contentment: "Not that I speak in regard to need, for I have learned in whatever state I am, to be content: I know how to be abased, and I know how to abound. Everywhere and in all things I have learned both to be full and to be hungry, both to abound and to suffer need. I can do all things through Christ who strengthens me" (Phil. 4:11-13).

First, Paul makes a declaration of *contentment* (Phil. 4:11) because the Philippians' revived support toward his ministry. Paul wants them to know that he is rejoicing in their commitment to the faith (Phil. 4:10), but that his contentment is not dependent upon it. Note that Paul never said "I am content," but rather, "I have learned." He had to go through the process of learning in order to reach his present state. Paul was an apostle, but he was also human, and he had to learn through life's struggles and discipline himself (1 Cor. 9:27). This statement is even more staggering in light of what Paul endured (2 Cor. 11:23-28). Stop and re-read the passage above, taking care to contemplate the great tribulations Paul experienced. In 2 Cor. 4:17, he mentioned his terrible suffering, but referred to it as "light affliction." Light! Can we really learn to have such contentment in the face of such torment?

Second, Paul lists the *conditions* in which he can be content (Phil. 4:12). Whether Paul was abased (i.e. brought low) or abounding; whether he was full or hungry; whether he had plenty or was lacking, Paul could be content because he was strengthened through Christ. The ASV translation of 4:12 is particularly intriguing: "In all things have I learned the secret." Possessing this mindset could be called a secret, as it seems not many possess it. But how could Paul make such statements about something that seems nearly impossible to achieve?

Third, Paul gives the *cause* for his contentment (Phil. 4:13), declaring that he could "do all things through Christ who strengthens" him. He did not have this state of mind before he was placed into Christ; he had to learn it and did so only through Christ. How can someone have such contentment through Christ? Because Christ assures us of eternal life, and if we follow Him, no one can rob us of that promise. Paul could be beaten, hungry, or imprisoned, yet still have that hope. Outside of Christ, we are left to depend upon external circumstances in the here and now for happiness, and when those are taken away, so is our contentment. Only in Christ can anyone hope for eternal life and possess the contentment that Paul describes.

PRESSING POINT:

Contentment can be found even in the midst of much tribulation. The problems of this life become small when one realizes all that Jesus provides.

PART TWO: THE PRACTICE

It is common in Paul's writings to have a doctrinal section followed by a practical section. For example, look at the book of Ephesians. In chapters 1-3, Paul presents the blessings of being in Christ, while in chapters 4-6, he explains *how* to live as a member of His body. Thus, he presents a doctrinal section (1-3), followed by a practical section (4-6). After we learn a truth, we then need to learn how to apply it. There are practical aspects in Part 1, but it primarily sought to present the truth, namely that the key to overcoming the plague of addiction and inheriting heaven is the gospel of Christ. Part 3 will delve deeper into the spiritual aspect, but Part 2 will explore more practical ways that have been successfully used to accomplish sobriety and improve lives. Are you ready to take action?

PART TWO: THE PRACTICE

7

ATTITUDE OF GRATITUDE

Have you ever considered the relationship between ingratitude and addictive behavior? Addiction involves engaging in compulsory actions despite the negative consequences. Addicts will readily throw away things for which they should be thankful simply for the instant gratification of "the high." Their families, friends, health, possessions, and future are all sacrificed. The addict may sincerely feel that s/he is thankful for the blessings in life, but his/her actions tell a different story. True gratitude is more than a feeling and requires more than saying, "I'm thankful." True gratitude is seen in your attitude; learning to have an attitude of gratitude is crucial to the foundation of a new life.

THE BIBLE & GRATITUDE

In examining Christian characteristics as revealed in Scripture, it is clear that an attitude of gratitude is vital to being a servant of Christ. Thanksgiving saturates the pages of Scripture. God provides the necessities of life for us and, for that provision, we are to be thankful. Jesus is recorded as giving thanks for food (Matt. 26:26; Mark 8:6; John 6:11, 23), even though he was the Creator of the world (John 1:1-5; Col. 1:15-17). Paul is also recorded as giving thanks for food and acknowledged that it ought to be received with thanksgiving (Acts 27:35; 1 Tim. 4:3). More importantly, he manifested an attitude of thanksgiving for God's grace and mercy (1 Cor. 15:57; 1 Pet. 1:3-5; Tit. 3:3-7; 1 Tim. 1:12-17). Thanksgiving is directly connected with acquiring the peace of God: "Be anxious for nothing, but in everything by prayer and supplication, with thanksgiving, let your requests be made known to God; and the peace of God, which surpasses all understanding, will guard your hearts and minds through Christ Jesus" (Phil. 4:6-7).

Here, Paul begins by admonishing his readers not to be anxious, and then makes a contrast between being anxious and praying to God with thanksgiving. But that is not all. He also uses "and" to join these two sentences together, which guarantees that God's peace will be with us. "The peace of God" is contingent upon our attitude of thanksgiving. How can you have inner peace if you are not a grateful person?

MAKING A GRATITUDE LIST

So what can you do to help become and remain grateful? We encourage making a daily gratitude list. It does not have to be in any specific order, like most to least important. It is recommended that you keep a notebook so that it will be organized and easily accessible. The following is an example list:

1. I am thankful for God (Father, Son, Holy Spirit).
2. I am thankful for my church family.
3. I am thankful for my wife, children, parents, rest of family.
4. I am thankful for my friends.
5. I am thankful for my health.
6. I am thankful for a place to live.
7. I am thankful for food.
8. I am thankful for my cat.
9. I am thankful for clothes.
10. I am thankful for a warm bed at night.
11. I am thankful for opportunities to help others.
12. I am thankful I don't have to participate in addictive behavior.

13. I am thankful for sunshine.

14. I am thankful for mountains.

15. I am thankful for the ocean.

16. I am thankful for green grass.

17. I am thankful for sunrise and sunset.

18. I am thankful for clouds.

19. I am thankful for music.

20. I am thankful for green pastures.

21. I am thankful for hills.

Notice the specifics of the list. A general item (e.g. God's creation) has been turned into several specific items; the more items on the list, the better. You can never be too grateful! We recommend truly pondering all that you have for which to be grateful. You will have the same items repeated over and over, day by day, but that is actually a great thing. Repetition is needed more than you think, especially in overcoming an addiction. Although there will be repetition of general items, you will also add more specific things that happen to you that should be included. Think about the "little things." Even when things go wrong, remember that it could always be worse; be grateful they are not. There will also be "big things" that happen, and you definitely want to record those. For example, getting a job or going back to school are great accomplishments. Especially important is working on mending relationships, for which opportunity you need to be particularly grateful.

It does not matter how bad you think your day is; you have so much for which you should be grateful. Recognizing this will help your attitude, and this is key. Anger all too often results in a relapse into addiction. What will help you with constructing your own gratitude list is consistency. It is easy to discontinue making these lists—very easy. It is a commitment you need to make and, more importantly, keep. Set a specific time to write your list; people are different, so pick the time that works best for you.

And remember, the list is for you and will help you only if you are willing to first help yourself.

In light of the connection between gratitude and prayer, it is important to give thanks to God often. Keep your list where it will be easily seen by you in order to remind you to maintain an attitude of gratitude. You could even put each day's list on the refrigerator so that you make a habit of reviewing your lists. Daily reminders of why you should be grateful will refocus your thoughts, making it hard to stay angry, depressed, or resentful. After all, how can you be imprisoned by fear or rage when looking through a notebook filled with reminders of all those reasons why you should be grateful.

A quick note, however, regarding the inclusion of possessions on your list: remember that the Bible does not praise the accumulation of trinkets. As was said in 1 Tim. 6:8: "And having food and clothing, with these we shall be content."

It seems many people are easily angered over petty, trivial things. All too often, people like to focus on the negative rather than the positive. But gratitude is a key, not only to your recovery, but also to your service to Christ.

PRESSING POINT:

*Begin to live like you are thankful for everything with which
you have been blessed. Remind yourself by making a list.
Think and pray about your list often.*

8

ACCOUNTABILITY PARTNER

Accountability is defined by Merriam-Webster as "the quality or state of being accountable; especially: an obligation or willingness to accept responsibility or to account for one's actions." People struggling with addiction are renowned for shirking responsibilities, ignoring obligations, and consequences, and being unwilling to accept accountability for their actions. Accepting responsibility is another part of the transformation you need to enact in your life if you are going to remove the chains of addiction. Having an accountability partner can help you begin to make that change.

NECESSITY OF AN ACCOUNTABILITY PARTNER

You are going to give an account to Christ for your deeds (2 Cor. 5:10). There is no way around it. Keeping this day in mind should make it harder to do wrong because it will ensure your mind is focused on the ultimate goal. However, at this crucial point in your life, it is important to have someone there to help motivate you to do what is right. Perhaps you have heard, "A friend in need is a friend indeed." An accountability partner is designed to help keep you on the right track. Note that I said *help*; the decision to stay on the right track is completely *yours*.

FINDING AN ACCOUNTABILITY PARTNER

How do you go about finding such a person? There are several characteristics vital to an accountability partner.

First, this person must be one of godly character, bound by biblical, moral principles. Remember, this person will not only help you through your struggle with addiction, but will also guide you toward heaven. Therefore, you need to pick someone who is on his/her way there, a person well known for faithfulness in worship and service to God. It should be someone who is responsible with money and, if married, in a visibly healthy marriage.

Second, an accountability partner needs to be someone with whom you feel comfortable, but not someone who will be untruthful. This person needs to tell you what you need to hear, not what you want to hear. If you are serious about recovering, you will not desire someone to "baby" you. The Bible maintains that someone who refuses rebuke or reproof is unwise (e.g. Prov. 1:30-33; 9:8; 13:1, 8; 15:31-32; 17:10; 24:25; 27:5). The "God breathed" Word, Paul said, "is profitable for doctrine, for reproof, for correction, for instruction in righteousness, that the man of God may be complete, thoroughly equipped for every good work" (2 Tim. 3:16-17). In order to be "complete," you must allow God's Word to reprove and correct you, even if it is through the instruction of people teaching it to you. Your accountability partner cannot hold you accountable if s/he does not help you improve, and there is no improvement without correction.

Third, this person needs to be someone to whom you are not sexually attracted. Why? Sexual attraction can be detrimental to your recovery. You need to concentrate on loving yourself before trying to love another; there needs to be no ulterior motive for selecting your accountability partner. It is all too easy, especially with a mind recently clouded and "re-wired" through addiction, to make a decision based upon the wrong reasons, and picking a partner based upon physical attractiveness is the wrong reason. Of course, you might try to convince yourself otherwise, thinking that you picked him/her for some other altruistic reason. Please, do not try and fool yourself. Hopefully, if you are not strong enough to avoid this temptation, then the person you approach will be mature enough spiritually to reject the request and explain why.

RELATIONSHIP WITH YOUR ACCOUNTABILITY PARTNER

What will your relationship with your accountability partner be like? Since s/he is working to hold you accountable, you need to contact him/her frequently. You need to let him/her know, preferably each day, that you have not "used." This will be a tremendous help on your road to recovery. You will be responsible for calling and informing him/her about your day, about your struggles, as well as your triumphs. You will have to commit to honesty, no matter what. Knowing that you will have to tell your partner if you "used" should help deter you from slipping back into old habits. Alone, it might not be enough to keep you from "using," but it will be an enormous help regardless.

One particular reason your accountability partner needs to be someone to whom you are comfortable expressing feelings is that you need to share your inventory list with this person. And you need to share it honestly. True is the saying "confession is good for the soul." Sharing your faults with another person is admittedly difficult, but necessary. It is, in fact, a biblical principle (Jas. 5:16; 2 Sam. 12:13). There are things you have done in the past that you view as horrendous and might make you feel like a horrible person; you may be ashamed to tell someone. Remember this in those dark times: you do not have to be that person any longer.

If you desire to change, you must be completely honest with yourself and others. If you are not honest with yourself, you will not be honest with your accountability partner, and the process will not work. Take inventory of your life and discuss it with your accountability partner, openly and honestly. You must leave the life of deception. It is time to clean house.

PRESSING POINT:

Learn to be accountable for your actions;
get help in the form of an accountability partner.

9

INVENTORY, PT. 1
RESENTMENTS

A n inventory is a checklist of what is "on hand." It is absolutely crucial that businesses take inventory so as to keep track of expenditures and profits; a business cannot be successful without taking inventory. As individuals, we need to do the same. Do you know what you have "stocked up" in your personal inventory? However long you indulged in addictive behaviors, you had your reasons; I might not know why, but you do. More importantly, you have the ability to examine yourself more closely than anyone else, and this is key to your success.

Search your feelings and your past. Have you stockpiled fears? Are you guilt-stricken by the harm you have done to others and/or yourself? Are you angry at yourself and others? All of these things can become a source of fuel as you begin to crash and burn.

What are your triggers? In other words, are there people, places, or situations that easily provoke you to slip back into addictive behavior? You must become aware of these in order to be prepared the next time you meet them, which means you must take a trip inside yourself and confront them. This is not an easy task, but it is a necessary one.

Notice again the words of Christ: "What comes out of a man, that defiles a man. For from within, out of the heart of men, proceed evil thoughts, adulteries, fornications, murders, thefts, covetousness, wickedness, deceit, lewdness, an evil eye, blasphemy, pride, foolishness. All these evil things come from within and defile a man" (Mark 7:20-23).

You need to first confront what is on the inside to effectively deal with what occurs on the outside. You need to tackle the "evil thoughts" stored within your mind because only then will you be able to actively seek change. People often revert to addictive behavior in response to fears, guilt, grief, anger, etc., rather than deal with any of them. It is easier to fall back into the comforts of habit, but this action is only an attempt to escape reality. Poised at the edge of sobriety and sin, you are faced with a choice: confront these issues or continue in the bondage of addiction. If you choose the first, then continue reading. If you choose the second, then put down this book and go indulge. We cannot choose for you. This is your choice.

RESENTMENTS

Although the Alcoholics Anonymous 12-step model is, in some ways, flawed (see Appendix A), there are some sound biblical principles contained therein. Step four, for example, states, "Made a searching and fearless moral inventory of ourselves."[1] The authors of the twelve steps also wrote, "Resentment is the 'number one offender.' When the spiritual malady is overcome, we straighten out mentally and physically."[2] This is a biblical principle. Resentment is defined in the *New Oxford American Dictionary* as "bitter indignation at having been treated unfairly," and from bitterness comes hate and anger. The Bible teaches that anger is not to be stored up within us. Solomon wrote, "Do not hasten in your spirit to be angry, For anger rests in the bosom of fools" (Eccl. 7:9). The meaning of "rests" carries a meaning of "to rest, settle down and remain."[3]

---

1. Alcoholics Anonymous, 3rd ed. (New York: Alcoholics Anonymous World Services, 1976), 59.

2. Ibid., 64.

3. *Enhanced Brown-Driver-Briggs Hebrew and English Lexicon* (Oak Harbor, WA: Logos Research Systems, 2000), 628.

Anger should not be sought, and when it arrives, it should be dealt with promptly. The man who allows it to "rest" is a "fool."

Paul taught something similar in his letter to the Ephesians: "Be angry, and do not sin: do not let the sun go down on your wrath" (4:26). In simpler terms, he was warning against going to bed angry. Paul also wrote, "Let all bitterness, wrath, anger, clamor, and evil speaking be put away from you, with all malice. And be kind to one another, tenderhearted, forgiving one another, even as God in Christ forgave you" (Eph. 4:31-32). We agree with the apostle and believe wholeheartedly that "resentment is the 'number one' offender."

Letting your resentment rest is dangerous; it risks you resorting back to addictive behavior and losing your soul. The Alcoholics Anonymous author wrote:

> In dealing with resentments, we set them on paper. We listed people, institutions or principles with whom we were angry. In most cases it was found that our self-esteem, our pocketbooks, our ambitions, our personal relationships (including sex) were hurt or threatened...On our grudge list we set opposite each name our injuries. Was it our self-esteem, our security, our ambitions, our personal, or sex relations, which had been interfered with?[4]

Here is something that will help you Press Forward in your recovery from addiction. First, make a list of people you resent; make note of the reasons why, including what they did/said, and how it affected you. Be honest with yourself. You may think it looks silly on paper, but resentment is more serious than you think. When writing these names down and analyzing (honestly!) why you feel the way you do, there should be a moment when you realize that you do not have to feel that way. You have chosen to be angry due to how you view the situation. Look at it now

---

4. Alcoholics Anonymous, 64.

in a different light, from the perspective of the very people you resent. There will always be situations that bring about anger. For example, if your spouse has an extra-marital affair, the love you have for him/her will bring on certain emotions—anger, jealousy, sadness—which are completely understandable. However, we never need to justify why we harbor anger and bitterness against someone. For one in your position (i.e. someone attempting to overcome addiction), this step is vital to recovery. Admittedly, having your spouse "cheat on you" is not easily swept aside, but it is crucial that you learn to view the situation from different angles. Study the following example:

Bob is mad at Sam because Sam slept with Bob's wife. Therefore, Bob resents Sam for being a jerk and ruining Bob's marriage. How could Bob view the situation differently? It takes two to have an affair. Two people fell into a sinful situation, not just Sam. Do you think Bob wants people holding grudges against him for his sins? Of course not. He reflects on the situation and realizes he has not been the husband he should have been. Resenting Sam will not help fix an obviously discontented marriage or repair a friendship; it will only make the situation worse. Bob discovers that he does not resent Sam, but rather desires that Sam find help with his problems.

Viewing such a situation in a different light is difficult, and requires great effort, but the rewards of doing so far outweighs the consequences of bottling up such feelings. Writing this inventory and honestly going over it with your accountability partner will help you deal with these feelings openly and honestly.

Study this second example of reviewing a situation in a different light. Joe resents the police officer who arrested him for drunk driving. Joe believes the cop had it out for him and treated him unfairly. How can Joe view the situation differently? Wasn't the cop just doing his job? Many, many, many lives have been lost because people have driven under the influence; cops are meant to protect and serve. Had Joe not been stopped and arrested, he could have killed someone. Getting arrested might even have saved his life. By looking at the whole picture, Joe is able to respect the cop for protecting the community.

Changing your view of a situation requires analyzing the situation honestly and without bias. Although this can be difficult, you need to be willing and committed to doing it.

Stephen Covey authored a stellar book entitled, *The 7 Habits of Highly Effective People*. In the book, he shared a situation in which he was on a subway and a man was sitting idly nearby while his children were being disruptive:

> I could not believe that he could be so insensitive as to let his children run wild like that and do nothing about it, taking no responsibility at all. ... So finally, with what I felt was unusual patience and restraint, I turned to him and said, "Sir, your children are really disturbing a lot of people. I wonder if you could control them a little more?" The man lifted his gaze as if to come to a consciousness of the situation for the first time and said softly, "Oh, you're right. I guess I should do something about it. We just came from the hospital where their mother died about an hour ago. I don't know what to think, and I guess they don't know how to handle it either."[5]

Wow! How do you respond to such a statement? Covey continued, "Suddenly I *saw* things differently, and because I *saw* differently, I *thought* differently, I *felt* differently, I *behaved* differently."[6] Paul described two characteristics of love: it "thinks no evil" and "believes all things" (1 Cor. 13:5, 7). Love motivates us to give other people the benefit of the doubt; it is not quick to assign blame or improper motives to someone. Love strives to wear the proper glasses.

We do not have to store anger; it is a choice. Make the list.

5.   Covey, *7 Habits*, 30, 31.

6.   Ibid.

PRESSING POINT:

It is important to examine yourself and make an inventory of resentments, then strive to change your feelings toward them.

10

PERSONAL INVENTORY, PT. 2
FEARS & TRIGGERS

In addition to resentments, we need to confront our fears. Many embrace addiction because they fear facing reality. What are you afraid to face? What are you afraid could happen to you? Why are you afraid of it? List your fears; bare them to the light.

Low-self esteem is a well-known companion of people enslaved by addiction. Rather than attempt to be successful in life, it is so much easier to find solace in a temporary high. Be honest with yourself and list your fears, along with why you think you have them. You may fear your spouse will leave you or that you will not find a job. You may fear your family will never forgive you or that you will live your life alone. List them and, as with everything on this inventory, honestly go over it with your accountability partner, discussing how to confront these fears.

You should include within the list of fears, or separately, a trigger list. A trigger is what it sounds like: it sets something off—you to be exact. Triggers refer to things that have the potential to provoke you to indulge in addictive behavior. Triggers can be people, places, or things that easily spark a desire to embrace the addiction. There are people with whom you participated in these behaviors and places in which you did them. Will going back to these places or being near these people help free you or recall you to your old habits? Different addictions may have different or similar triggers. For example, Dr. Jerry Martin stated, "Those struggling with pornography will find particularly challenging: internet access, times of boredom or tiredness, and aloneness."[1] There are countless things that can bring your addictive behavior back to the forefront of your mind. Do not do this to yourself. Avoid these triggers, for they are the past.

As Peter said, "For we have spent enough of our past lifetime in doing the will of the Gentiles—when we walked in lewdness, lusts, drunkenness, revelries, drinking parties, and abominable idolatries. In regard to these, they think it strange that you do not run with them in the same flood of dissipation, speaking evil of you" (1 Pet. 4:3-4).

Peter speaks of people who still participated in these worldly activities, thinking "it strange" that those who once participated in such things no longer do. The word "strange" carries a meaning of "to surprise or astonish by the strangeness and novelty of a thing; to think strange, be shocked."[2] The Gentiles were enslaved by worldliness and were surprised that someone turned from such pleasures. They speak "evil of you" because they do not understand and choose instead to judge. This shows their selfishness. They want you to be right there with them, embracing the world (cf. 1 John 2:15-17).

We all have these type of people in our lives; who are they in yours? List their names and why they are triggers. Rather than dealing with each person as you encounter him/her, develop a plan of action, so that *when* you do come into contact, you will be prepared. Just planning to avoid them is not sufficient. You do not need to live in fear of running into them.

There are also places and things that your mind heavily associates with your addiction. The obvious places are bars, clubs, drug dealer's houses, homes of friends where you "partied," etc. Write down all these places and how you will go about avoiding them. One thing that really sticks out in my mind are specific songs associated with the addiction. There are likely songs that you enjoyed listening to while indulging in the

---

1. This quote is from the written interview conducted with Dr. Martin, which is in chapter 1.

2. Thayer, *Greek-English Lexicon*, 432.

behavior, songs that promote drug use, fornication, etc., and now they forever remind you of substance abuse. Vulgar, filthy music needs to be avoided anyway if you desire to follow Christ, but it may very well be that a "clean" song takes you back to your addiction. Make a list of such songs; do not intentionally listen to them, especially not early in this process. It is recommended that you listen to these songs and/or discuss them with your accountability partner early on and work on viewing the songs differently. Listening to these songs alone could be dangerous and drag you right back into the pit.

Times of the day, and certain days of the week or month could all be triggers and your accountability partner needs to know them. They cannot help you learn to deal with these triggers if they do not know what they are. Think of the activities you associate with your addiction. For example, it is common for people to drink beer while fishing. I know of a man who did not eat pizza for years simply because he used to drink beer with it, and pizza resulted in his craving beer. You know your triggers. List them. We do not have to hide anything from the world in the recovery process. Having a list of triggers helps prepare you to face anything and everything in recovery. You do not have to live a life without fishing or eating pizza, but you do need to be honest in recognizing these triggers and properly learn how to overcome them.

If you are struggling with pornography addiction, then the internet would be a serious trigger. Do not be naive about it, thinking, "I can handle it." There is good "accountability software" out there, one of which is Covenant Eyes. Discuss this with your accountability partner because s/he needs to have free access to the sites you visit. If you are married, your spouse definitely needs access. Soberly contemplate the words of Jesus: "If your right eye causes you to sin, pluck it out and cast it from you; for it is more profitable for you that one of your members perish, than for your whole body to be cast into hell. And if your right hand causes you to sin, cut it off and cast it from you; for it is more profitable for you that one of your members perish, than for your whole body to be cast into hell" (Matt. 5:29-30).

Finally, list the people you have wronged through your unhealthy behavior. Why? Because more likely than not you harbor guilt over what you have done, and that guilt has the potential to hold great power over you. Face what you have done to these people and know there is a loving God who desires to forgive you. I assume since you are going through this book that you do not want to commit such acts against people anymore. If that is the case, list these people and be willing to confront your actions. Instead of letting what you have done eat you from the inside out and hinder your progress, face it and press forward. Paul wrote, "Brethren, I do not count myself to have apprehended; but one thing I do, forgetting those things which are behind and reaching forward to those things which are ahead, I press toward the goal for the prize of the upward call of God in Christ Jesus" (Phil. 3:13-14).

Paul was able to move on from his past, not that he never thought about it (1 Tim. 1:12-17). He had faced it and refused to let it hinder his moving forward. Those past actions cannot be undone; you need to face them, accept them, and move forward so that you can effectively serve Christ. This list is crucial, and we will come back to it again in later chapters.

PRESSING POINT:

Our personal inventory ought to include fears, causes of guilt, and a list of what triggers our urges, along with a plan to avoid them.

11

DAILY INVENTORY

Suppose you buy a new car but you never change the oil, rotate the tires, or replace the brakes. Contemplate how dependable the vehicle will be for you. The owner's manual contains important sections on maintenance and troubleshooting, as the makers of the vehicle realize the necessity of continual maintenance. Think about this. Cars are temporary in the grand scheme of things. Humans, on the other hand, were created in the image of God (Gen. 1:26-28; Psa. 8:4-6), and possess a soul, which is worth far more than a car (Matt. 10:28; 16:26). Therefore, what sense would it make to keep up maintenance on a car only to neglect maintenance on your life? If you desire your life to be in good working order, then you need to provide the proper maintenance. Create a daily inventory, and follow it on a repeated basis.

The principle of a daily inventory derives from the tenth step of Alcoholics Anonymous: "We continued to take personal inventory and when we were wrong, promptly admitted it." Any follower of God's Word should do the same. Maturing spiritually is challenging and requires genuine effort, especially after having your mind corrupted by harmful addiction. There is one key characteristic here: humility. Vital to this continual inventory is the admission of any and all wrongs. Pride is the direct opposite of humility and is a barrier to spiritual growth. Your accountability partner needs to be someone who will point out wrongs in your life when necessary and, even more important, you need to allow him/her to do it.

The Proverbs writer labels someone who refuses reproof as a fool. It is possible that you do not realize that you did something wrong; your partner is there to help you recognize it. In that instance, you need to heed the reproof and admit fault, as refusing to do so hinders forgiveness (1 John 1:9). Being "clothed with humility" (1 Pet. 5:5) is demanded of all Christians and is especially crucial in overcoming addiction. Your accountability partner should help keep you in check with your humility and you need to let him/her.

You need to look inside yourself and see whether you are living a Christ like life. Paul wrote, "Examine yourselves as to whether you are in the faith. Test yourselves. Do you not know yourselves, that Jesus Christ is in you?—unless indeed you are disqualified" (2 Cor. 13:5). A life of addiction is chaotic, lacking responsibility. Train yourself to plan your days each morning or, better still, at the beginning of every week.[1] Figure out what works best for you, write down what the day(s) might bring, and examine how you should handle it. This will help guard against acting in a way you should not. The end here is not merely to cease "using," but rather to live a life consistent with biblical principles. At the close of each day, reflect on all you said and did, then ask questions like, "Did it go well? Why?" "What went wrong? Why?" "Where was I resentful or selfish?" "Was I kind, giving, etc.?" For example, use the following list as a blueprint for daily reflection:

- Situations I handled poorly and why.
- Situations I handled well and why.
- Resentments I developed and why.
- People whom I learned need help, which I can provide.
- Did I waste time or was I properly productive?

---

1. Covey, *7 Habits*, 146-182.

- Did I crave that substance/behavior today? In what situation did those cravings arise?
- Did I meditate on God's Word today?

This is a general sample of what you need to review. You want to deal with your past, not forget it. Everything we do, right or wrong, teaches us a lesson if we are willing to listen. Remembering what did not work will help you stay on the right track in the future. Paul understood this, for he remembered he was "chief of sinners" (1 Tim. 1:15). Remembering what you were will help keep you from being that person again. Use the inventory of the past to help with your new, daily inventory. Be diligent in your records and reflection, and look for similarities in behavior; you cannot fix a problem unless you are first aware of it.

PRESSING POINT:

Living a sober and righteous life requires routine maintenance one day at a time. Strive for honest self-evaluation and a humble heart of acceptance.

12

MAKING AMENDS

Being enslaved by a harmful addiction can easily leave a path of wreckage behind you, one upon which others might get hurt, both physically and emotionally. Fixing our mistakes may not be as easy as clicking the "undo" button, but we do not have to allow our past actions or inactions to destroy us. This step has the potential to be "nerve racking," so why even bother? Two reasons. First, it is biblical. Second, it will lead to inner peace.

THE BIBLE AND AMENDS

Making amends is a biblical principle present in both Testaments. It first appears in the Law of Moses, wherein it is recognized that harm done to an individual requires restitution be made to the one wronged:

> And the Lord spoke to Moses, saying: "If a person sins and commits a trespass against the Lord by lying to his neighbor about what was delivered to him for safekeeping, or about a pledge, or about a robbery, or if he has extorted from his neighbor, or if he has found what was lost and lies concerning it, and swears falsely—in any one of these things that a man may do in which he sins: then it shall be, because he has sinned and is guilty, that he shall restore what he has stolen, or the thing which he has

extorted, or what was delivered to him for safekeeping, or the lost thing which he found, or all that about which he has sworn falsely. He shall restore its full value, add one-fifth more to it, and give it to whomever it belongs, on the day of his trespass offering."

Lev. 6:1-5

The same theme continues with the prophet Ezekiel: "Again, when I say to the wicked, 'You shall surely die,' if he turns from his sin and does what is lawful and right, if the wicked restores the pledge, gives back what he has stolen, and walks in the statutes of life without committing iniquity, he shall surely live; he shall not die. None of his sins which he has committed shall be remembered against him; he has done what is lawful and right; he shall surely live" (Ezek. 33:14-16).

Observe now two examples from the New Testament. The Law of Moses was still in effect while Jesus lived and its teachings permeate the writings of the apostles. Luke 19:1-4, for example, tells of a man named Zacchaeus who desired to see Jesus and even climbed up into a tree to see Him. Jesus calls out "Zacchaeus, make haste and come down, for today I must stay at your house" (Luke 19:5), and so the man "made haste and came down, and received Him joyfully" (19:6). What is significant in this passage is that the people thereabouts complained that Jesus was going to stay with "a sinner" (19:7), for they considered Zacchaeus a traitor to his own people, being a tax collector for the Romans, even though he was, himself, a Jew.

What this story tells us is that it does not matter what you have done in the past; Jesus wants to save you! Zacchaeus' desire to live right encompassed a desire to make amends with those he had wronged. "Then Zacchaeus stood and said to the Lord, 'Look, Lord, I give half of my goods to the poor; and if I have taken anything from anyone by false accusation, I restore fourfold'" (Luke 19:8). A desire to follow Christ includes a desire to make possible restitution and be willing to right any wrongs where possible. In Zacchaeus' case, he repented of his corrupt actions of the past and hoped to make restitution with the people he had cheated.

The second instance of amends in the New Testament concerns a Philippian jailor. As mentioned in chapter six, Paul and Silas were beaten and put into prison for helping someone (Acts 16:16-24). God in His power made a way for Paul and Silas to be released, and the jailor, noticing they had left, was going to kill himself; prisoners escaping on a guard's watch meant execution for that guard (16:25-27). Paul, however, stopped him from taking his own life, and the jailor wanted to be saved (16:28-30). After having the gospel preached to him and his household, the jailor "washed" the wounds of Paul and Silas (16:31-33). The jailor's desire to follow Christ included a desire to make amends to Paul and Silas; he could not "undo" the beating, but he did "wash their stripes."

BEGINNING THE PROCESS

In desiring to follow Christ, you will seek to make amends with those you have wronged. This is no easy task; it is a challenge emotionally and mentally, but the reward far outweighs the cost. The key question you should be asking is how to go about making amends. When writing out your personal inventory, you made a list of people you have wronged and shared this list with your accountability partner. Go back over this list with him/her and seek counsel as to how to approach making amends. You need to exercise caution and proceed wisely. Do not dive into this step without first consulting your accountability partner, who should be a spiritually mature Christian. There may be people who would seek to harm you if you approached them, and in such cases, you may want to send a letter or call first before approaching personally. For instance, you may have had an extra-marital affair with someone; the situation could get ugly quickly, as a marriage and family are involved, rather than a single person. These situations demand caution and wisdom. In the case of an affair, your duty is to make amends with your own spouse. Take responsibility for your actions, but do not approach these matters in such a way that you will cause more harm than good.

Whatever your task, make sure you handle it according to biblical teaching. Seek counsel from a solid Christian counselor. If you have stolen money and are able to pay it back, then do so. There is a good chance your addiction has cost your parents and family members a lot of money. Seek to make it right. If you are now living with your parents, but have a job, pay them rent. "But they didn't ask for it," you say. Pay them rent anyway. This is not about waiting for people to ask you for restitution, but rather about being prompted to make amends by your desire to follow Christ. So go through this list with your accountability partner and begin the process of making amends.

Remember, this is a *process*, and it is very easy to let guilt eat away at you. It will be easy to let this list overwhelm you and, while contemplating what you have done, think that you do not deserve to be saved. If you think you do not deserve to be saved, *you are absolutely right.* That is why Christ left glory (John 17:5) and died for you. Never forget that. By God's grace, you have an opportunity to change your life. Move forward in this endeavor to the best of your ability and, during it, know that you are striving to do right. When feelings of depression and guilt start to weigh you down, contact your accountability partner or a faithful Christian immediately. You may even have to consult a Christian counselor. The path to amends will be challenging, but the reward is precious.

PRESSING POINT:

"Making amends" or "making restitution" whenever and wherever possible is both an appropriate and biblical answer to those whom we have wronged.

13

HAVING A VISION

There is a story told of a wise Native American father who wished to give his property and possessions to one of his three sons—more specifically, to the one who showed the most prowess and promise. As a test, he pointed to a mountain sitting bold against the sky and sent his sons toward it, asking each to bring back a token to show how far up the mountain he climbed. The first one returned with a white wild flower in his hand; the father knew that it grew just above the timberline. The second one returned with a red flint stone, which revealed to the father that he had almost made it to the top. The third son was gone for a long time and returned empty-handed. "Father, where I went," he explained, "there was nothing to bring back, but I stood at the summit and looked out upon the valley where two great rivers join the ocean." The proud father said to him, "It has been the ambition of my life that one of my sons should see what you have seen. You have nothing in your hands, but you have a greater thing—a vision in your soul. This is the greatest gift of all!"[1]

* * *

Stephen R. Covey shared a powerful exercise, which we now ask you to do: Picture yourself driving to a funeral parlor or chapel. As you walk

---

1. This illustration was obtained from a sermon by George Bailey.

down to the front of the room and look inside the casket, you suddenly come face to face with yourself. This is your funeral, three years from today. There will be four speakers reading over your body. Now, think deeply: what would you like each of these speakers to say about you and your life?[2]

It is possible for you to live in such a way that you can have exactly those things said about you. Covey calls this principle, "BEGIN WITH THE END IN MIND." You need to make sure you live in such a way that it leads you to the desired destination: heaven. Living with structure and organization is challenging but worth it. It is no accident that successful people are organized and structured. They do not "wing it" through life. Having a vision truly entails having the dedication to follow through with it.

PERSONAL MISSION STATEMENT

Covey discussed what he called "A Personal Mission Statement."[3] This concept is indeed powerful and, most importantly, biblical *when done correctly*. It would be easy for you to write out a statement that focuses on worldly gain or popularity, but we are challenging you to write a statement that aligns with biblical principles. Paul wrote, "For to me, to live is Christ" (Phil. 1:21). Think about that statement: Paul's life *was Christ*. Whether he did or did not do something was based upon his relationship with Jesus Christ. Your mission statement needs to be led by the Bible and, therefore, will be Bible-centered.

The concept of "Roles And Goals," also developed by Covey, consists of breaking down the statement, "into the specific role areas of your life and the goals you want to accomplish in each area."[4] For example: Husband (Wife), Father (Mother), Son (Daughter), Employee, Student, Friend, Member of a particular community organization, etc. Notice "Christian" is not on the list of roles. Why not? Because being a Christian is not a

---

2.   Covey, 7 *Habits*, 97.

3.   Ibid., 106.

4.   Ibid., 136-37.

separate role, but rather dictates how you live in all areas of life. Thinking of it as a separate role is incorrect, as Christ must be "our life" (Col. 3:4). Write down how you will lead your life in each of these areas according to biblical principles. How will you live so that you "let your light so shine before men, that they may see your good works and glorify your Father in heaven" (Matt. 5:16)? How will you work so as to reflect a biblical work ethic and earn money so that you may provide for family and those in need? How will you study with a thirst for knowledge that you may use it to the glory of God? If you are married, we recommend that you and your spouse develop a marriage mission statement together, focusing on how each of you live as a spouse so as to bring honor to God. How will each of you live as a spouse so as to have a divorce-proof marriage? If you have children, how will each of you live so as to provide your children with godly teaching/examples?

Here is an example of a biblically focused mission statement:

Personal Mission Statement

The identity of "Christian" will permeate my life. God's Word will dictate how I live in every role, and I will not allow anything to deter my service to Jesus. I will remain faithful to Him. I will edify my brothers and sisters and teach others the gospel/help people in need.

Husband/Wife

I will fulfill the role of husband/wife as set forth in Scripture. I will seek to understand his/her feelings and seek his/her best interest. I will forever remain faithful to him/her. I will be financially responsible.

Father/Mother

I will fulfill the role of father/mother as set forth in Scripture. I will not only teach my children to live according to the gospel, but I will also provide a godly example.

Son/Daughter

I will fulfill the role of son/daughter as set forth in Scripture. I will be honest to my parents and honor them for life. I will care for them in old age.

Employee/Employer

I will fulfill the role of employee/employer as set forth in Scripture. I will be honest about working my agreed upon hours. I will not do anything, even if commanded, to compromise my integrity. I will not ridicule other employees. I will give everyone the benefit of the doubt and give my best. I will seek to teach the gospel to those around me.

Student

I will fulfill the role of student according to principles set forth in Scripture. I will respect my teachers and strive to complete, to the best of my abilities, my assignments. I will not be ashamed to confess my beliefs to students and teachers.

Friend/Neighbor

I will not gossip or backbite. I will treat others the way they should treat me according to God's Word. I will be a dependable person to the best of my ability. I will help others who are in need.

Clearly, this is a generic example of a mission statement. It is up to you to personalize it and make it your own. The main objective is to let the Bible dictate what you write.

THE BIBLE AND VISION

Many people possess vision, in that they have end goals in mind and are dedicated to living in such a way as to achieve them. However, we are not only advocating vision, but also, and more specifically, biblical vision.

The folly of not having God in your vision is clearly shown in Scripture. There are two key passages that teach this concept.

First, there is the "certain rich man" who was concerned about storage space for his crops (Luke 12:16-17). His solution was to "pull down my barns and build greater" (12:18). Notice his fatal flaw: "And I will say to my soul, 'Soul, you have many goods laid up for many years; take your ease; eat, drink, and be merry'" (12:19). Such an attitude is to be possessed only if there is no resurrection of the dead, as Paul explains in 1 Cor. 15:32. In other words, there is purpose to this life, and it involves the life hereafter. To possess an "eat, drink, and be merry" attitude is to ignore our true goal and not possess biblical vision. Thus, God said to this certain rich man: "Fool! This night your soul will be required of you; then whose will those things be which you have provided?" (Luke 12:20). Jesus concludes with: "So is he who lays up treasure for himself, and is not rich toward God" (12:21). This rich man did not possess true vision.

In the second example of biblical vision, James describes someone who does not include God in his plans (James 4:13-17). This man describes a goal of selling things and making profits, but never mentions God. We could not even do such things without the Creator, and to disregard Him in our actions is the height of arrogance: "Instead you ought to say, 'If the Lord wills, we shall live and do this or that.' But now you boast in your arrogance. All such boasting is evil" (Jas. 4:15-16). The man in this example boasted out of pride and inflated self-worth; he did not possess true vision because he could not see God's rightful place as the orchestrator of all things. Thus, James concludes, "Therefore, to him who knows to do good and does not do it, to him it is sin" (James 4:17). To exclude God from our vision is sin.

You can live your life with biblical vision and purpose, but only if you believe you can.

PRESSING POINT:

Important to any achievement (including sobriety) is to have a clear vision of where one is headed and to have goals ready to get you there, all of which are centered upon Jesus Christ.

14

ACHIEVING THE VISION

N one of us would have much sympathy for someone who is given a great opportunity, but does nothing with it. Think of a recent high school graduate who receives a full ride to a prestigious college, only to drop out in the second semester or squanders the four years partying. Now picture someone who realizes he needs to have a biblical vision but does nothing to achieve it. Realization is only the first step towards possessing the vision; you then need to take the subsequent, logical steps toward achieving it. This chapter discusses the importance of spending your time wisely and gives practical suggestions on how to make every second count while seeking your own personal, biblical vision.

IDLE HANDS

There is an old saying, "Idle hands are the devil's playground." You probably already know how valid a statement this is, but did you know that the Bible teaches this principle as well? For an example, read this passage regarding young widows: "And besides they learn to be idle, wandering about from house to house, and not only idle but also gossips and busybodies, saying things which they ought not" (1 Tim. 5:13). Here, the women's idleness contributed directly to their sinfulness. Now study the solution Paul proposed: "Therefore I desire that the younger widows marry, bear children, manage the house, give no opportunity to the adversary to speak reproachfully" (1 Tim. 5:14). The solution here is action. It is all too easy to succumb to vice when bored; laziness and sloth are gateways, in and of themselves, to committing other sins. "See then that you walk circumspectly, not as fools but as wise, redeeming the time, because the days are evil" (Eph 5:15–16). Redemption bears the idea of "mak[ing] wise and sacred use of every opportunity for doing good, so that zeal and well doing are as it were the purchase money by which we make the time our own."[1] Only "fools" sit in idleness; the "wise," however, take action and commit every second of every day to God's glory.

In connection, Dr. Martin emphasized the importance of preventative measures, citing the importance of "reduc[ing] times of vulnerability, get[ting] involved in alternate activities, schedul[ing] personal family devotionals, and stay[ing] engaged with trusted accountability mentors and sage counseling."[2] If you are active and busy, your mind will have no opportunity to linger on old habits and dependencies. What follows are suggestions on how to avoid idleness and make every moment count towards developing your own biblical vision.

REDEEMING TIME

You need to create goals consistent with your biblically aligned vision. Before addressing these, however, you are cautioned against wasting time or spending it in harmful ways. You are no stranger to vice and understand the futility of lost chances. The Bible outright condemns laziness (cf. Prov. 6:6-11; 10:26; 12:24, 27; 13:4; 20:4; 21:25; 26:16; 2 Thess. 3:10-12). There is a time for rest and relaxation; in fact, it is necessary for good health. Rest and action, however, require a balance. We live in an electronic age. There are so many positive achievements technology has provided, but they also have the potential to trap us in idleness. Hours

---

1. Thayer, *Greek-English Lexicon*, 220.

2. This quote is from the written interview conducted with Dr. Martin which can be viewed in chapter 1.

spent in front of the T.V., computer, or game station could be detrimental not only to your health, but your spiritual well being as well.

You need to establish a strong work ethic. You need to be dependable. Learn to schedule your days or, at the very least, your weeks. Write down all of your priorities and schedule them accordingly. I am writing as someone who (apparently) had an innate fear of making a weekly schedule. "Winging it" is neither wise nor productive; scheduling, whether daily or weekly, is crucial to organizing your time and avoiding idleness.

The following are ideas that you can incorporate into your life. These suggestions may not be applicable to everyone, but should act as general guidelines for filling your time with positive and healthy activities.

Study/meditate upon the Bible

The Bible is our guide (Psa. 119:105) and your key to recovery (Psa. 119:11), as well as heaven (John 12:48). Avoid waiting until the end of the day to read/study; we are too tired, both physically and mentally, to focus all of ourselves then. Choose the most convenient time in your schedule to meditate upon God's Word. There are many great study aids available, all of which would serve you well on the road to recovery.

Get out of debt

I am not a professional financial expert, but there are many practical ways offered by such people to help someone struggling with debt. Getting out of debt will not only relieve you of stress, it is also a biblical principle: "The wicked borrows and does not repay, but the righteous shows mercy and gives" (Psa. 37:21). We refer you to Dave Ramsey's website, which is full of sound financial advice, and pays particular attention to the "debt snowball." When addressing your debt issues, make a written budget. Organize and label envelopes for gas, food, electric bills, etc., and put the appropriate amount in the correct envelope each month. This exercise will help you organize finances, as well as your mind, and provide a sense of satisfaction as your debt slowly decreases.

Find employment

If you are already employed, ask yourself if there are any triggers associated with that job. Did you include these when writing your inventory? If not, do so now and discuss them with your accountability partner. Is that job a threat to your recovery? Do you need to leave and find new employment? For example, if you are a recovering alcoholic who works at a bar or a nightclub, you may be making the healing process more difficult. Employment in such places is not consistent with living the Christian life and is a direct impediment to you finding an addiction-free path.

The Bible emphasizes a strong work ethic, so if you are unemployed, start looking for work. You need to be honest with yourself here. Are you ready to handle money on your own? Can you juggle the chaos of rent, bills, and the multitude of other living expenses? If you need to be in an in-house facility ("halfway house") temporarily, where your money is controlled for you, then do so. It could be that you have such a place close to you that would be willing to handle your money for a time. We highly recommend Project Rescue for just this purpose. Whatever your situation, you must be honest with yourself. In looking for employment, it is recommended that you visit the nearest job center and obtain information about how to dress and act during interviews, how to write resumes, etc. There is no shame in seeking help; these centers and professionals are there to offer advice and guide you along.

Go to school/educate yourself

"I can't go back to school; I'm not smart enough; I'm too old to start learning new things." Are these excuses familiar? You do not have to go to school, but if you have a desire to, then pursue it. This new path, however, should not be approached immediately. Undertaking formal education is a decision weighted with a great deal of responsibility, and you need to be ready to shoulder that burden before attempting to return to school or enrolling for the first time. If you physically attend classes on a campus, you will most likely be confronted with triggers. There are many options for online classes, which could remove potential stressors, like commuting and scheduling, and new triggers that come with course loads and social stimuli. Discuss these possibilities with your accountability partner and with college graduates. Exercise patience in achieving this goal; it is a big step, and you need to be ready for it. Perhaps you never graduated high school, and college is a few steps ahead of where you are right now. Start small instead, and set a goal to obtain your GED. Maybe you are interested in learning, but not formal education itself; educate yourself through regular study (textbooks, journal articles, blogs, podcasts, etc.). Do not allow the pursuit or absence of an education hinder your service to Jesus.

Volunteer/help others

Nursing homes, hospitals, children's homes, libraries, and many other places take on a variety of volunteers. This would be a great opportunity for you. Not only would you be avoiding idleness, but you would also be helping others, which is key to avoiding depression. Call such facilities in your area; find one that most suits you and where you will be able to do the most good. After all, serving Christ is about helping others (Luke 10:25-37; Gal. 6:10; Jas. 1:27).

Organized volunteering is not the only way you could give back to the community. Think of people in your area you could visit, such as the elderly or sick. If you know a widow/er or elderly couple who is paying someone to mow their yard, volunteer to do it for free. If you live in an area where people do not have their trash picked up by the city, then volunteer to take it to the local dump. Send cards, not just on holidays, but randomly throughout the year. Most importantly, be kind to others.

Obtain healthy hobbies

Potential hobbies could be almost anything. Is there something you used to enjoy doing, but abandoned when your addiction took over? If so, incorporate it back into your life. If you enjoy playing chess, think about starting a chess club in your community. Choose a sport you enjoy and start playing. Some communities have softball leagues or other intramural sports. Crucial to a healthy lifestyle is exercise. You do not need to be an inactive person. It may be that your job consists mostly of sitting at a desk or a lot of driving; incorporate exercise into your life. Be active and you will become too busy and preoccupied to think of former bad habits.

PRESSING POINT:

Idle time is a dangerous enemy to sobriety. By learning to schedule your time and stick to it, you can eliminate this danger.

15

HEALTH & NUTRITION

This chapter is designed to give you some simple tips and practical advice to help you begin your healthy lifestyle, as well as to provide biblical insight on the matter. I am not a professional nutritionist, a registered dietician, or a professional trainer. However, this is a topic that I have researched and taught regularly at an alcohol and drug treatment facility. Professionals in this field will direct you to the appropriate resources required for adopting a new, healthy lifestyle.

HEALTH AND SOBRIETY

You may ask, "Why is there a need for such a chapter in this book?" We believe many people fail to see the connection between living a healthy life and staying sober. Your eating habits are actually connected to recovery from your addiction. Dr. John Newport wrote a book entitled, *The Wellness-Recovery Connection*, in which he shows the direct link between staying sober and living a healthy lifestyle. The old saying, "You are what you eat," really does have merit. What we eat affects how we feel. It is very easy to swap addictions, as it were, and trade off alcohol or other drugs for sugary, processed food. Avoiding overeating is, naturally, very important, but so is *what* you eat. You can consume fewer calories, but if you consume junk, you will negatively affect your health. "Skinny" is not always healthy. The following are some practical tips to get you started:

- Limit sugar intake; try Stevia, local raw honey, and coconut sugar.
- Avoid (or at least limit) soda consumption.
- Avoid processed food as much as you possibly can.
- Check nutrition labels; if you can't pronounce it, you probably don't want to eat it.
- When grocery shopping, stick to the perimeter; processed and sugary foods are in the center aisles.
- Cook with healthy oils, like grape seed or coconut oils.
- Eat your veggies! They are crucial to a healthy diet.
- Eat snacks like nuts, fruits, hummus, etc., instead of chips or candy bars.
- Avoid fried food; grill, roast, or bake instead.
- Eat more chicken, fish, and turkey.
- Buy healthy cookbooks/follow blogs for healthy recipe ideas.

If you have ever been to a 12-step meeting, there was likely coffee there. It seems coffee is the favorite drink of those who have recovered from alcohol addiction. This can, however, present a problem. As Dr. Newport stated, "Caffeine is an extremely powerful stimulant that serves to overstimulate the adrenal glands and elevate blood-sugar levels, causing a quick energy rush that is shortly followed by a 'crash.'"[1] Dangerous to an addict's recovery, particular from drug-use, is the fact that "in large doses, caffeine produces symptoms similar to amphetamine and cocaine intoxication, with an associated development of tolerance and physical dependency."[2] The brain of one addicted to stimulants, such as cocaine, recognizes that a stimulant is being put into the body, which could trigger a craving for a stimulant in no way related to coffee. Are we saying you must eliminate all caffeine from your life forever? No, but we are saying that it certainly needs to be limited. Try some of the following:

---

1. John Newport, *The Wellness-Recovery Connection* (Deerfield Beach, FL: Health Commnications, 2004), 51.

2. Ibid., 52.

- Drink no more than two cups of a caffeinated beverage a day.
- Switch to decaf wherever possible, remember that even decaf has some caffeine.
- If currently consuming too much caffeine, do not cut it from your diet suddenly; gradually decrease over time until you either limit your caffeine intake or eliminate it completely.

What about exercise? Exercise is important for your overall health, but also for your mood. You may have heard of serotonin, which is a chemical in your body that greatly affects mood. Low levels often result in chronic depression. Exercise is one of several ways to naturally elevate serotonin levels. One registered dietician wrote:

> Approximately 75 percent of this chemical is located in cells of the gut, where it regulates intestinal movements. The rest is synthesized in neurons of the brain; it's here that serotonin influences mood. High levels are associated with an elevated mood while low levels are associated with depression. Though many neurotransmitters work in harmony to influence mood, serotonin is one of the most important. Its levels are influenced by external factors, such as sunlight, diet and exercise.[3]

Notice the three "external factors" that influence serotonin levels: sunlight, diet, and exercise. Living a healthy lifestyle contributes to feeling better, which in turn aids your recovery from addiction. You may be prone to diving into exercising heavily, but we advise that you first consult a physician and maybe even a professional fitness trainer.

When it comes to exercise, what are your options? There are two main forms of exercise: cardio and strength. Cardio relates to the heart and is designed to raise the heart rate through activities like walking,

---

3. Michele Turcotte, "The Effects of Exercise on Serotonin Levels," http://www. livestrong.com/article/22590-effects-exercise-serotonin-levels.

running, swimming, jumping rope, etc. Strength training does not focus on increasing the heart, but rather the muscles. It includes weight lifting, pushups, resistance band training, etc. Regarding serotonin levels, "walking, running, biking, swimming (among others) seem to be the most effective at increasing serotonin synthesis in the brain."[4]

Develop a fitness schedule and choose days and times to exercise. Different times work better for different people, so plan according to what works for you. Learn what is best for your body and take it slowly; you are trying to retrain your body, as well as your mind. Remember to consult your physician about an exercise program that suits you best.

THE BIBLE & HEALTH

Many fail to see the connection between living a healthy life and serving God, but there is a connection. Logically speaking, the healthier we are, the more we are able to serve God. Scripturally speaking, we are created in the image of God and are stewards of the bodies God has given us. Paul actually referred to the individual body of the Christian as "the temple of the Holy Spirit," and commanded us to "glorify God in your body" (1 Cor. 6:19-20). The context concerns fornication, but the underlying principle is that glorifying God with our bodies requires properly caring for our bodies.

John wrote to Gaius, "Beloved, I pray that you may prosper in all things and be in health, just as your soul prospers" (3 John 2). At least two important lessons are learned from this verse:

- Physical health is important, and it is right to pray for it.
- We should not allow taking care of physical health to hinder our spiritual health. John conditioned praying for his physical health with "as your soul prospers." If the soul is not prospering, then being in great physical health is superfluous.

---

4. Ibid.

Our society is plagued with overeating and unhealthy diets, which too many disregard. It may be surprising to some that the Bible does indeed address this issue. Solomon wrote, "Do not mix with winebibbers, Or with gluttonous eaters of meat; For the drunkard and the glutton will come to poverty, And drowsiness will clothe a man with rags" (Prov. 23:20-21). Notice that "gluttonous eaters of meat" are associated with "winebibbers," both of which reveal a lack of the self-discipline necessary for the true Christian life (1 Cor. 9:27; Gal. 5:23). Earlier, in the same chapter of Proverbs, we read, "When you sit down to eat with a ruler, Consider carefully what is before you; And put a knife to your throat If you are a man given to appetite. Do not desire his delicacies, For they are deceptive food" (Prov. 23:1-3).

Solomon uses very vivid language to describe the harm of overeating. The word "desire" originally expressed the idea of coveting or lusting after. Do not lust after food, or you will be consumed with that desire. Self-control at the dinner table is a seemingly neglected biblical principle. Chasing after one's selfish desires, including over indulging in food, does not align with biblical principles (Phil. 3:19; 1 Cor. 6:12) and is not good for your health. As Solomon warned, "Have you found honey? Eat only what you need, That you not have it in excess and vomit it" (Prov. 25:16). It makes sense that the first-century church fasted often, as it helps one with self-control, a necessary Christian trait (Acts 13:1-3; 14:23; 27:33; 1 Cor. 7:5).

PRESSING POINT:

Health and nutrition play a key role in staying sober. What you eat or drink, how often, and how much can affect your mood in the same way mood-enhancing drugs would.

PART THREE: THE DOCTRINE

Ronnie Crocker, program manager for Project Rescue, once said something to me along the lines of, "I do not want people to get sober and go to hell." That statement made an impact upon me. Becoming sober and overcoming addictive behavior is a beautiful thing. However, there is a bigger picture here. You can discontinue a harmful habit and still be lost. The following section teaches you how to have sins forgiven through Christ and remain faithful to Him.

16

BIBLICAL AUTHORITY

The role of authority is best understood by first examining the absence of it. Most likely, you have lived your life in a state of anarchy, with a lack of authority or with yourself as the sole authority. The *New Oxford American Dictionary* defines "anarchy" as "a state of disorder due to absence or nonrecognition of authority." But what is the result of an "absence or nonrecognition of authority"? It is a state of disorder. A society without governing bodies would be a scary situation. Imagine no police or fireman, no mayors, governor, or president. The immediate absence of politics might sound like a relief, but what would it truly be like? Civil authority is, at its core, a positive concept; it commands and enforces that which is right.

What about authority in religion? Is there a standard we must follow or can we do whatever we see fit?

The first sentence in the Bible sets forth, in no uncertain terms, that we are subject to God's authority: "In the beginning God created the heavens and the earth" (Gen. 1:1). God's creative power demands His authority and our obedience. After creating man, God gave him instructions. Why? Because God is Creator and, therefore, has authority over Creation.

Psalm 19:1-6 also declares God's creative power and then he exalts His Word (19:7-14). Why? Because His creative power demands His authority. This principle permeates the pages of Scripture (e.g. Psa. 95-96; Isa. 40; Rom. 1:18-32). I once heard it said in a sermon, "Do you want to make your own rules? Then go create a universe and make them." It is a valid and an incontrovertible truth.

THE "CHAIN" OF AUTHORITY

When studying authority in religion, it is helpful to think of it as a chain, with each subsequent link an authoritative source to obey. The chain is as follows: The Father—the Son—the Holy Spirit—the Apostles—the Written Word.

The Authority of the Father

God sent His Son into this world, which was necessary for the forgiveness of our sins (John 3:16). In taking on flesh and being begotten of the Father (John 1:1-3, 14), Jesus submitted to the will of His Father. Jesus, during His earthly ministry, affirmed on several occasions His submission to His Father:

- "All things have been delivered to Me by My Father, and no one knows the Son except the Father. Nor does anyone know the Father except the Son, and the one to whom the Son wills to reveal Him" (Matt. 11:27).
- "I have come in My Father's name, and you do not receive Me; if another comes in his own name, him you will receive" (John 5:43).
- "This commandment have I received of my Father. ... The works that I do in My Father's name, they bear witness of Me. ... My Father, who has given them to Me, is greater than all; and no one is able to snatch them out of My Father's hand. ... Many good works I have shown you from My Father" (John 10:18, 25, 29, 32).

The Authority of Christ

Just as Christ affirmed the authority of God, so too did the Father recognize the authority of Christ, His Son. One such occasion is found in the Transfiguration. Jesus's appearance changed before the eyes of the apostles (Matt. 17:2). When Moses and Elijah appeared, Peter wished to "make here three tabernacles" (Matt. 17:3-4). But the Father made it known that Jesus was on a higher plane than them. He spoke from heaven, "This is My beloved Son, in whom I am well pleased. Hear Him!" (Matt. 17:5). Before Jesus ascended back to heaven to reign over His kingdom, He declared: "All authority has been given to Me in heaven and on earth" (Matt. 28:18), and then He ascended to take the throne (Acts 2:30-36; Heb. 1:1-3). At the end of days, it will be Christ's words that ultimately judge us (John 12:48).

The Authority of the Holy Spirit

Jesus promised His apostles that He would send the Holy Spirit to guide them "into all truth" (John 16:13). This promise is recorded elsewhere (e.g. Matt. 10:19, 20; Luke 24:44ff; Acts 1:4-8) and is a further sign of the authority passed from the Father to Jesus, and, in turn, to the Spirit so as to guide the Apostles "into all truth." What the Spirit would reveal was called "all truth" and, therefore, directly derived from the all-knowing authority of the Father.

The Authority of the Apostles

The apostles, as recorded in Acts 2, received the Holy Spirit's guidance as promised. Luke writes the phrase, "apostles' doctrine" (Acts 2:42), not because the doctrine originated with the apostles, for they were humans and not deity, but because they taught through the inspiration of the Holy Spirit. Paul wrote "that the things which I write to you are the commandments of the Lord" (1 Cor. 14:37). The apostles were able to teach and lead with authority, because the Spirit led them "into all truth."

If Christ was the right hand of God, then the apostles were the fingers working individually, though together, to a common, holy end.

The Authority of the Written Word

The Father—the highest authority—gave Jesus the authorization to speak in His name. Jesus then sent the Spirit upon the apostles, which inspired the apostles to provide a written message for us. This message is the "all truth," God's Word about which Jude aptly wrote, "the faith which was once for all delivered to the saints" (Jude 3).

Paul affirmed the "mystery" (gospel) and that it was written for all "partakers of the promise in Christ Jesus" (Eph. 3:6). These signs were "written that you may believe that Jesus is the Christ" (John 20:30, 31). God intended for His message to be delivered to us in an understandable, written form; why else would he entrust His Word to men? Today we can preach and teach with authority, just as the apostles did in the first century, because we have the written authority from God. After all, it was "His divine power [that] has given to us all things that pertain to life and godliness, through the knowledge of Him who called us by glory and virtue" (2 Pet. 1:3).

LACK OF RESPECT FOR BIBLICAL AUTHORITY TODAY

The present religious scene can be very discouraging. There are thousands of denominations with dissenting traditions and ever-multiplying opinions. Who is right and who is wrong? Can we know for certain one way or another? John removed all doubt, as he wrote:

> Now by this we know that we know Him, if we keep His commandments. He who says, "I know Him," and does not keep His commandments, is a liar, and the truth is not in him. But whoever keeps His word, truly the love of God is perfected in him. By this we know that we are in Him. ... By this we know that we love the children of God,

when we love God and keep his commandments. For this is the love of God, that we keep his commandments. And his commandments are not burdensome. ... These things I have written to you who believe in the name of the Son of God, that you may know that you have eternal life, and that you may continue to believe in the name of the Son of God.

1 John 2:3-5; 5:2-3, 13

"His word" is the standard by which "we know." The key to respecting His authority is being intellectually honest with the text of the Bible. Imagine a mother telling her child to clean his room. What if he interpreted her command like this: "I don't think my mother really meant for me to clean my room. She'll still love me, even if I don't." Is this child being honest about what his mother said, or is he attempting to make the command suit his personal preference?

We all face barriers when trying to be honest with what the Bible tells us is right and wrong. Even the most concrete and unequivocal lessons can be blurred by emotion, society, and other external factors.

Family

There are those who will not be honest with the text because of family tradition. My parents never did it that way, so why should I? They fool themselves into believing that they will be "okay" going down that same path. Just because your family chooses a particular way does not make it correct. Admittedly, it is difficult to separate yourself from family and habit, but we must always remind ourselves of who has *the* authority? Soberly contemplate these words of Jesus: "Do not think that I came to bring peace on earth. I did not come to bring peace but a sword. For I have come to 'set a man against his father, a daughter against her mother, and a daughter-in-law against her mother-in-law'; and 'a man's enemies will be those of his own household.' He who loves father or mother more than

Me is not worthy of Me. And he who loves son or daughter more than Me is not worthy of Me" (Matt. 10:34-37).

Religious Groups

There are many who will not be honest with the text because of faithfulness to a group or person. Saul left the Jewish religion to follow Christ, even though it meant developing enemies among his former brethren (Acts 9:1-25), because he was honest with the evidence before him. Some people seem to blindly follow what a religious leader says without searching the Scriptures for themselves (Acts 17:11). Paul made it clear that the servant is nothing, for it is only "God who gives the increase" (1 Cor. 3:5-9; cf. 1 Cor. 1:10-17; 4:6-7). Our allegiance is to Christ, not to people.

Happiness

There are many who will not be honest with the text because being happy requires breaking a law of Christ. Whether it is indulging in alcohol, fornication, or any other number of temporal pleasures, there are those who allow their personal happiness to blur the teachings of Scripture. We are called to deny ourselves and submit to Christ. Period (Matt. 16:24-26). True contentment lies only in Christ (Phil. 4:11-13), not in fulfilling our own selfish, physical desires.

Conscience or Emotions

Emotion can be a strong instigator of the actions we choose to take. God's Word is the standard for knowing one is saved, not some feeling or sensation of salvation. If emotions are allowed to become the standard, then the authority of God's Word will be shunned and religious confusion will result. If everyone determined his salvation based upon feelings, then everyone would "feel" himself to be saved! There has to be an absolute standard and God's written Word is it. In Acts 8:35-39, the

Ethiopian eunuch rejoiced because he knew he was saved, as he heard the gospel and obeyed. Saul, who would later become Paul, "lived in all good conscience before God" (Acts 23:1) while persecuting "this Way to the death" (22:4). According to his conscience, Paul was right before God, but he was not saved until Jesus forgave him; and he was not forgiven until he had complied with the Gospel (Acts 9; 22:3-21; 26:1-23).

IMPLICATIONS FOR BIBLICAL AUTHORITY

What does all of this mean? It means consequences; positive ones if authority is respected, but negative ones if authority is disregarded. All of us will stand before Christ to be judged by His Word (John 12:48). We have been told what the standard is and, therefore, how we ought to live to prepare for the Judgment. This means accepting what the Bible teaches as authoritative. God has provided us with an inerrant, harmonious gospel.

PRESSING POINT:

God is absolute, therefore, God's Word is also absolute.
The Bible, God's Word, is thus the standard of authority.
You must be willing to overcome any and all barriers
to accept that incontrovertible authority.

17

GETTING TO KNOW GOD

G od is Spirit (John 4:24) and eternal (Psa. 90:2). He is omniscient (all-knowing) (Matt. 10:29, 30), omnipotent (all-powerful) (Job 38), and omnipresent (all things are before Him) (Prov. 15:3). A study of God's nature is indeed a rich and rewarding one. When studying His nature, it is crucial to realize that all of His characteristics rise and fall together; no one trait can stand alone or be separated from any other. Moreover, it is necessary to emphasize two characteristics of God: love and holiness.

GOD'S LOVE

It is rather fascinating how the Bible connects God and love. The Bible does not just say that God has love, but rather that He *is* love (1 John 4:8, 16). He is the essence of love, and whether something "is loving" is determined by the nature of God. We must not only understand that "God is love," but how His love was manifested to us. "In this the love of God was manifested toward us, that God has sent His only begotten Son into the world, that we might live through Him. In this is love, not that we loved God, but that He loved us and sent His Son to be the propitiation for our sins" (1 John 4:9-10).

God's love entails helping others, but what loving others actually means is all too often confused in today's society. Love is perceived as a subjective feeling and that love of something is based solely upon how we feel about it, rather than upon God, who is love. Society views love as tolerating sinful behavior and that it is unloving to bring to someone's attention to his sinful conduct. Biblical love, however, does what is necessary to help others, even when it involves pointing out sin.

In what is recognized as the great chapter on love (1 Cor. 13), Paul describes how love behaves. Love keeps the welfare of others in mind and never intentionally does anything to bring harm to another. Love is unselfish. Earlier in the Corinthian letter, Paul addressed the situation of a brother living in fornication. Many today would affirm that a person's sexual lifestyle is no one else's business and that it would be unloving or even arrogant to publicize it. But Paul actually referred to the Corinthian brethren as arrogant for ignoring the situation (1 Cor. 5:1-2). Our society, according to Paul, has it backwards. Whereas bringing sin to one's attention can be done in an unloving manner (Eph. 4:15), the act itself is, in actuality, one of love. Love desires everyone to go to heaven and, therefore, will warn others of sin. God's love for us was perfectly exemplified in Christ, who warned us of the consequences of sin (John 8:24), simply because of His love for us.

GOD'S HOLINESS

One cannot truly understand God's love without understanding His holiness. The existence of God demands absolute morality. What is right and wrong flows from the nature of God. He inherently cannot tolerate that which is unholy, for God is holy (1 Pet. 1:16). Is God love? Absolutely. Does God overlook sin? Absolutely not. Many act as if they can live in direct violation of God's will while still being saved, simply on the basis that "God is love." Such is a gross misunderstanding of what love means.

Both the Old and New Testaments reveal God's punishment of people for disobeying Him. For example, Uzzah was struck dead by the Lord for touching "the ark of God" (2 Sam. 6:1-8). This may seem harsh, as he only touched it in order to keep it from hitting the ground. However, God had previously instructed the "who and how" of transporting the ark, namely who was allowed to move it and how, and had given a warning of death to anyone else who touched it (Num. 4:1-15). Did God's love cancel out His holiness? Did God stop being love when He struck Uzzah dead? To ask is to answer: God's Holiness demands that He cannot ignore rebellion.

The New Testament records the instance of Ananias and Sapphira. They "sold a possession" and affirmed that they gave the entire price to the apostles, when they actually "kept back part of the proceeds" (Acts 5:1-2). In so doing, they lied to the Holy Spirit/God (5:3-4), and He struck them dead (5:5-10). God's holiness would not allow their sin to be overlooked, and this display caused great reverence for Him. Rather than hindering church growth, it actually contributed to it.

IMPLICATION

Part of God's love for us entails His warning of that which is wrong. Why is the Bible filled with commands not to participate in certain things? It is for the same reason a parent tells a child not to touch a hot iron or stick a fork in a socket. God does not want us to experience the punishment that will result from sinning, but do not think He will stop it from happening. In fact, His holiness demands punishment for wrongs committed. God created us as free moral agents able to choose the path we take. If God cannot be loving without warning us of evil and telling sinners they are wrong, then how can we be loving without warning people about sin and allowing the gospel to open their eyes to the fact that they are living in sin?

In the end, when we are judged (Heb. 9:27; 2 Cor. 5:10; John 12:48), do you think we will "slide by," having neglected God's commands?

PRESSING POINT:

God's love does not cancel out His holiness,
but rather they exist in harmony. Obedience is necessary.

18

DIFFERENCE IN THE TESTAMENTS

Have you ever wondered why there are two testaments in the Bible? There is a reason, for God does nothing arbitrarily, and understanding it is key to understanding the Bible.

THE PURPOSE OF THE LAW

What was the purpose of the Law of Moses? Jeremiah, an Old Testament prophet, informs us that the Law of Moses was never meant to be permanent, for there would come a time when it would no longer be effective. He was very specific, in that he said God would "make a new covenant with the house of Israel and with the house of Judah," which would be different than "the covenant that I made with their fathers in the day that I took them by the hand to lead them out of the land of Egypt" (Jer. 31:31-32). Take note of what we learn from this prophecy:

- The covenant was not meant to be permanent; God planned to make a new one.
- The new covenant would be different from the one made with Moses.

Jeremiah said that the new covenant would be made "with the house of Israel and with the house of Judah," but he is not referring to the Jewish nation (Rom. 2:28-29; Gal. 6:16). Under the new covenant, physical nationality makes no difference. So we learn from Jeremiah that God never meant for the Law of Moses to be permanent and that the physical nation of Israel would be replaced with a spiritual nation under the new covenant.

It is this prophecy that the writer of Hebrews applied to the covenant of Christ (Heb. 8:6-13). Paul addresses the purpose of the law in the letter to the Galatians, asking the question: "What purpose then does the law serve?" He answers: "It was added because of transgressions, till the Seed should come to whom the promise was made" (Gal. 3:19). Notice two things from this verse:

- The law was made because of sin, to reveal it, and to show its ugliness (Rom. 3:20; 7:7).
- The law was only to last until "the Seed should come," "the Seed" being Christ.

Paul expounds upon this point: "But before faith came, we were kept under guard by the law, kept for the faith which would afterward be revealed. Therefore the law was our tutor to bring us to Christ, that we might be justified by faith. But after faith has come, we are no longer under a tutor" (Gal. 3:23-25).

The very purpose of "the law" was "to bring us to Christ." "The faith," or gospel, has been revealed, and "we are no longer under a tutor." "The law" has served its purpose. The law was a "shadow" (Col. 2:17; Heb. 10:1) pointing to the perfect law of Christ, the gospel. If the law's purpose was "to bring us unto Christ," and He has come, then we cannot any longer be bound by the Old Testament laws. Christ affirmed that he did not come "to destroy the Law or the Prophets," but "to fulfill" them (Matt. 5:17). The next obvious question, therefore, is how was the law fulfilled?

FULFILLMENT OF THE OLD COVENANT

John 4:20-24 records Christ's explanation to the Samaritan lady that the time was coming when worship would not be according to the Law of Moses, but rather "in spirit and truth," according to a new covenant. Before Jesus ascended to heaven, He told His apostles, "These are the words which I spoke to you while I was still with you, that all things must be fulfilled which were written in the Law of Moses and the Prophets and the Psalms concerning Me" (Luke 24:44). Jesus was preparing people for the coming kingdom (Matt. 4:17; Mark 9:1; Luke 16:16).

It is the blood of Christ that fulfilled the old law (Matt. 26:28-29). His blood "nailed" the law "to the cross" (Col. 2:13-17). The purpose of the old law was to bring us to Christ, in whom we would be freed of sin. The death of Jesus Christ therefore fulfilled all that was foretold about the coming Messiah and ushered in a new age (Luke 24:44-49).

ESTABLISHMENT OF THE NEW COVENANT

The Hebrews writer said, "For where there is a testament, there must also of necessity be the death of the testator. For a testament is in force after men are dead, since it has no power at all while the testator lives" (Heb. 9:16–17). This is not a foreign concept; we all understand that a person's "Last Will and Testament" does not take effect until after his/her death. Additionally, it does not take effect the minute the person dies. After burial and a brief time of mourning, the family is called together, the will is read, and then it is legally ratified.

When was Christ's will ratified? The new covenant had to have a beginning, and that point was the day of Pentecost, following the resurrection of Christ (Acts 2; see chapter twenty for a full explanation). Animal sacrifices, religious feast days, Sabbath keeping, etc., were no longer required (cf. Col. 2:14-17). God's chosen people would instead be governed by the gospel of Christ (Acts 2:42), and from Acts 2 onward, we see God's people following the new covenant.

The establishment of the new covenant demands authority over us today. Therefore, it is vital that we "rightly divide the word" (2 Tim. 2:15) and not attempt to bind any aspect of the Law of Moses upon us today. It is an abuse of the Old Testament to bind ourselves to the Law of Moses, for the New Testament has been established and the Old fulfilled.

NEED TO STUDY THE OLD TESTAMENT

It has been said that the Old Testament is the New Testament concealed, and that the New Testament is the Old Testament revealed. The two go "hand in hand," and even though the old law has been fulfilled, the Bible student should also study the Old Testament. There are key reasons why this is so important:

- To learn of God's holiness (e.g. Exod. 19-20).
- It contains examples for us to follow (e.g., Rom. 15:4; 1 Cor. 10:6, 11; Heb. 11).
- It makes us "wise unto salvation" (2 Tim. 3:15), because it points to the Savior.
- It contains the story of Creation and the institution of marriage (Gen. 1-2).
- The miracles recorded therein confirm God's power (e.g. 1 Kings 18).
- The bold and powerful proclamations of the inspired prophets (e.g. Dan. 2:24-49).
- It contains prophecies of Christ and His church, and affirms His Deity (cf. Gen. 3:15; Isa. 2:2-4; 6:1-5; 7:14; 9:6; 53; John 12:41; 2 Sam. 7:4-17; Psa. 110; Acts 2:34-35). Note: Jesus is the very theme of the Old Testament, and He is found in every book.
- It is quoted/referenced abundantly in the New Testament (e.g. just read Hebrews).
- It teaches us the diabolical ways of our adversary (Gen. 3; Job 1-2).

- It contains eternal moral truths which will strengthen a Christian in His service to Christ and his treatment of others (e.g. Proverbs).
- It teaches powerful principles of prayer and worship (e.g. Psalms).
- Finally, and quite simply, because God revealed it to us (2 Tim. 3:16-17; 2 Pet. 1:19-21).

A proper knowledge of the Old Testament will cause the sincere Bible student to recognize its purpose and the need to study it.

PRESSING POINT:

Jesus fulfilled the old covenant and established His covenant with His blood. We are bound by this, not the Law of Moses.

19

GETTING TO KNOW JESUS

Jesus is easily the most influential figure in the history of the world, but who is He? To learn of Him, you must consult His Word. However, Jesus is not found in the pages of the New Testament alone: He is the theme of the entire Bible, which is a book about salvation, and Jesus is the Savior. As the previous chapter showed, the very purpose of the Old Testament was to point to and prepare for Jesus. So we must ask, "Who is He?"

HE IS GOD

Let's go with John back to the beginning. John wrote: "In the beginning was the Word, and the Word was with God, and the Word was God. He was in the beginning with God. All things were made through Him, and without Him nothing was made that was made" (John 1:1-3). "The Word" here refers to the pre-incarnate Jesus, that is, to His state before He lived on the earth in flesh (John 1:14). Jesus is deity; He is God, but not the same person as God the Father. He was with God, and He also was God, in that He possessed the same nature. He is a member of the Godhead (Matt. 28:18-20; Col. 2:9). There never was a time when Christ did not exist.

HE IS SAVIOR

The most popular verse in the Bible declares Jesus as Savior (John 3:16). In order to save us, He had to be crucified and raised from the dead (1 Cor. 15:1-4). The very purpose for God sending His Son was for Him to "save His people from their sins" (Matt. 1:21). If man could save himself, Jesus never would have had to leave the glory of being with God to come to this sin-stricken world (John 17:5). Man needed—and still needs—a Savior because "the wages of sin is death" (Rom. 6:23).

HE IS KING

After He was raised from the dead, He ascended to heaven to take the throne as King over His kingdom. This was Peter's message on that great day of Pentecost (Acts 2). Jesus had previously told Peter He would give him "the keys of the kingdom of heaven" (Mat. 16:19), which Peter used on that glorious day of Pentecost when people were added to His kingdom for the first time.

While on earth, Jesus prepared people for His kingdom. He gave a series of parables pertaining to it (Matt. 13); He taught how people are expected to live as citizens of it (Matt. 5-7); He predicted it was "at hand" (Matt. 4:17; cf. Mark 9:1); and He even spoke of its nature while on trial before Pilate saying, "My kingdom is not of this world. If My kingdom were of this world, My servants would fight, so that I should not be delivered to the Jews; but now My kingdom is not from here" (John 18:36). Only citizens of His kingdom will be saved (Col. 1:13).

HE IS PROPHET

Moses, in prophesying of the coming Christ, referred to Him as "a Prophet" (Deut. 18:15-18), which Peter confirmed was the coming of Jesus Christ (Acts 3:22-24). Prophets were spokesmen for God, and indeed, Jesus, God in the flesh, spoke the will of His Father (John 6:38; Heb. 1:1-4).

HE IS THE CHRIST, THE SON OF THE LIVING GOD

Jesus once asked Peter, "But who do you say that I am?" In reply, Peter attested, "You are the Christ, the Son of the living God" (Matt. 16:15-16). Christ is a title rather than a name. It describes who He is, namely the one chosen to come to earth and die for our sins. In being born of a virgin, He became the Son of God (Luke 1:35). Jesus had no earthly father, as He was begotten of God, His Father. In order to be saved by the Son of God, one must first believe in Peter's confession. We must believe that Jesus is the Christ, and Son of the living God.

HE IS HIGH PRIEST

The book of Hebrews sets forth reasons why the new covenant surpasses the old covenant, and the writer affirms that Jesus is superior to all who came before Him. One argument set forth is that of Jesus being High Priest (Heb. 2:16-18; 4:14-16; 7). Under the Law of Moses, only priests could enter into the Holy Place of the Tabernacle/Temple or into the Most Holy Place. The Holy Place pointed to the church, while the Most Holy Place pointed to heaven. Under the new covenant, however, all Christians are priests (1 Pet. 2) and Jesus is our High Priest. As the book of Hebrews plainly affirms, Jesus had to take on flesh, be tempted as man, and die for our sins in order to be our High Priest. He did, and He now reigns as our High Priest in the Most Holy Place, heaven.

HE IS JUDGE

Jesus came into the world to save (John 3:17), but the day will come when Jesus will be arrayed as Judge, and only those who have lived according to His standard will be saved. He plainly stated, "He who rejects Me and does not receive My sayings, has one who judges him; the word I spoke is what will judge him at the last day" (John 12:48). Paul referred to this as "the judgment seat of Christ" (2 Cor. 5:10), from which the One who shed compassion while on earth will pronounce Judgment on that final day.

He is eternally God, He died to save you, He reigns as King, He is the Prophet of whom Moses spoke, He is our High Priest, He is the Christ, the Son of the living God, and He will judge us on the last day. Understanding all this, why would you hesitate to serve Him?

PRESSING POINT:

Jesus is God, Savior, King, Prophet, the Christ, the Son of the living God, High Priest, and Judge. Submit to Him.

20

HIS CHURCH

Have you ever heard, "Give me Jesus, but not the church"? Is it even possible to have Jesus without the church? The problem comes with an ill-defined and a misunderstood concept of what the church really is.

The Greek word, which we translate as "church," originally referred to an "assembly" or "gathering" of people. The word is even used to refer to Israelites before Jesus ever built His church (Acts 7:38). So when the church is discussed in Scripture, it simply refers to an assembly of people belonging to Christ—those who have been "called out" of the world (cf. Eph. 2; Col. 1:13; 1 Pet. 2:9-10). The word is used in Scripture with three primary implications:

- Universally: "And he is the head of the body, the church: who is the beginning, the firstborn from the dead; that in all things he might have the preeminence" (Col. 1:18; cf. Mat. 16:18).

- Locally: "Unto the church of God which is at Corinth, to them that are sanctified in Christ Jesus, called to be saints, with all that in every place call upon the name of Jesus Christ our Lord, both theirs and ours" (1 Cor. 1:2; cf. Rom. 16:16).

- An Assembly: "For first of all, when ye come together in the church, I hear that there be divisions among you; and I partly believe it" (1 Cor. 11:18; cf. 4:17).

THE BODY

The word "body" is used interchangeably with "church," as Paul makes abundantly clear in his writing (Eph. 1:22-23; Col. 1:18). Christ's body contains those people who have been purchased with His blood (Acts 20:28). People become members of it when they comply with the terms of His gospel (discussed more in the next chapter). Paul affirms several key concepts regarding the body (church) of Christ.

Christ has authority over His church

- He is the Head (Eph. 1:22; Col. 1:18), and His headquarters are in heaven (Col. 3:1).

- There is one body (church) (Eph. 4:4), and no head has two bodies. So it is with Jesus: He only has one body (comprised of local churches), which is united through "one faith" (Eph. 4:5).

- Jesus is the authority over His body (Matt. 28:18-20; Col. 3:17) because He is Head, so all authority for the church must come from Him, that is, His Word (cf. John 12:48).

- His church is subject to Him (Eph. 5:24); you cannot properly submit to Him outside of His body.

- His church is His bride (Eph. 5:23-33; 2 Cor. 11:2), which Paul likens to a husband/wife relationship.

Salvation is only in the church

- Jesus Christ died for His church (Acts 20:28; Eph. 5:25); His blood purchased His church, and His blood is essential to salvation (Matt. 26:28). Therefore, the saved are in His church (body).

- Jesus loves His church (Eph. 5:25); He shows the ultimate love, and we must respond by submitting to Him in His body.

- Jesus is the Savior of His church (Eph. 5:23) and His body; therefore, He cannot be your Savior if you are outside His body.

- Reconciliation with God is in His church (Eph. 2:16); we are "reconciled unto God in one body by the cross," that is, brought to a proper relationship with the Father through the cross of Christ.

- The called are in His church (Col. 3:15). We are called by the gospel (2 Thess. 2:14), and the called are only in His body; you cannot be saved through the gospel without being in His body.

God receives glory in the church

- God's wisdom is made known by the church (Eph. 3:10), by "powers in heavenly places" (likely angels) through the church.

- His church is according to the eternal purpose of God (Eph. 3:11) and His eternal plan. Therefore, it is necessary.

- God is glorified in the church Jesus built (Eph. 3:21); Christians are to glorify God (1 Cor. 6:20; 2 Pet. 3:18) and God is glorified in the body of Christ.

- His church is glorious (Eph. 5:27), which is evident simply after learning about it.

IDENTIFYING THE BODY

How is His assembly to identify itself? It is common for a church to meet in a building and to have a sign outside identifying that particular assembly of people. The building and sign are optional, for the body of Christ can meet anywhere to worship Him, but it is helpful to identify the nature of the assembly through advertisements. Does the name by which the assembly identifies itself matter? Well, if the church belongs to Christ, then it follows that the church should bear a name that honors Christ. There is a mindset, prevalent today, that suggests the name of a church does not matter. This is erroneous, both logically and biblically. Logically, if the name does not matter, then it could be called *anything*, even the church of Satan, and to admit that it could not be called this one name is proof that the name matters.

Biblically, the church is given certain designations, and being Scriptural, they honor Christ, as He is the owner. Here is a collection of several such designations given to His church in the Bible:

- "church of God" (Acts 20:28; 1 Cor. 1:2; 1 Cor. 10:32; 1 Cor. 11:22; 1 Cor. 15:9; 2 Cor. 1:1; Gal. 1:13; 1 Tim. 3:5)
- "house of God" (1 Tim. 3:15)
- "church of the living God" (1 Tim. 3:15)
- "church of the firstborn" (Heb. 12:23)
- "kingdom of his dear son" (Col. 1:13)
- "body of Christ" (1 Cor. 10:16; 12:27; Eph. 4:12)
- "his body" (Eph. 1:23; 5:30; Col. 1:24)
- "household of faith" (Gal. 6:10)
- "household of God" (Eph. 2:19)
- "churches of Christ" (Rom. 16:16)

These designations identify an assembly as belonging to Christ, rather than identifying an assembly with a particular doctrine or practice. We desire to simply be Christians (Acts 11:26), members of the family of God. And you should make certain that you are in such an assembly or body (church) of Christ, as one cannot be saved outside of it.

PRESSING POINT:

Jesus purchased His church (assembly) with His blood, and you must be in that body in order to be saved by His blood.

<h1 style="text-align:center">21</h1>

SALVATION IN HIS CHURCH

Before reading any further, we ask that you first write down answers to these questions:

- Are you saved?
- If so, when were you saved?
- How were you saved?
- Have you been baptized?
- If so, how were you baptized (water sprinkled/poured on you; immersion)?
- Were you saved before or when you were baptized?

Since salvation is in the body (church) of Christ (Eph. 5:23), then one would need to be placed into that body in order to be saved. But when did that body begin? What did people do to become members?

THE BEGINNING OF HIS CHURCH

The apostles were promised by Jesus to be "endued with power from on high" by "the Holy Spirit," and they were told to wait in Jerusalem where this would occur (Luke 24:49; Acts 1:4-8). This power would bring forth the kingdom of Christ (Mark 9:1). The terms "kingdom" and "church" are used interchangeably. For example, Jesus said He would build His church, and then He noted that He would give Peter "the keys of the kingdom of heaven" (Matt. 16:18-19). The kingdom was to come with power, and the power came on the day of Pentecost following the Lord's resurrection, as recorded in Acts 2. This is the day His church began. Observe the following:

- The *power* from the Holy Spirit came (Acts 2:1-4).

- The *place* was Jerusalem (Acts 2:5).

- The *preacher* was Peter (Acts 2:14).

- The *prophecy* of Joel and David was confirmed by Peter, referring to that day and to the kingdom (Acts 2:16-36).

- The *pardon* (i.e. deliverance) was received by calling on the name of the Lord (Acts 2:21, 38-47).

This is the first day anyone was added to His church; it was the beginning of the new covenant of Christ, the gospel age. On this day, some 3,000 souls were added to His body (Acts 2:42, 47); they were placed into Christ, which is equal to being in His body (church). They heard the gospel preached with the affirmation that "God has made this Jesus, whom you crucified, both Lord and Christ" (Acts 2:36). They believed the gospel, and asked, "Men and brethren, what shall we do?" (Acts 2:37). Peter replied, "Repent, and let every one of you be baptized in the name of Jesus Christ for the remission of sins; and you shall receive the gift of the Holy Spirit" (2:38). He quoted Joel as well, saying, "And it shall come to pass That whoever calls on the name of the Lord Shall be saved" (2:21). He told them to "call," and then told them how to do so (Acts 2:38). Notice the parallels:

Acts 2:21	Acts 2:38
"whoever"	"every one of you"
"calls"	"repent and be baptized"

Acts 2:21	Acts 2:38
on the name of the Lord	in the name of Jesus Christ
shall be saved	for the remission of sins

Repentance, to which the next chapter is devoted, and baptism are required in order to obtain the "remission of sins." The Greek word, which we translate as "baptism" refers to a submersion or immersion, and the Scriptures describe it as being buried in water (Matt. 3:16; Acts 8:38-39; Rom. 6:3-4; Col. 2:12). An examination of Acts 2 reveals that those added to the church (2:42, 47) were not added until they were baptized. Salvation is found in the body of Christ, and faith, repentance, and baptism are doors into that body (cf. 1 Cor. 12:13). If salvation is in His body, and baptism puts one into His body, then baptism is essential to salvation. The following chart illustrates the connection between baptism and salvation. Please open your Bible and carefully read these passages.

Mark 16:16	baptized	—>	saved
John 3:5	born of water and the Spirit	—>	enter the kingdom of God
Acts 2:38	baptized	—>	for the remission of sins
Acts 2:41, 47	baptized	—>	added to the church
Acts 22:16	baptized	—>	wash away your sins
Rom. 6:3	baptized	—>	into Christ Jesus; into His death

Rom. 6:4	baptism	—>	into death; walk in newness of life
Eph. 5:26	with the washing of water by the word	—>	sanctify and cleanse
1 Cor. 12:13	baptized	—>	into one body
Gal. 3:27	baptized	—>	into Christ
Col. 2:12	baptism	—>	raised with Him through faith in the working God, who raised Him from the dead
Tit. 3:5	through the washing of regeneration and renewing of the Holy Spirit	—>	he saved us
1 Pet 3:21	baptism	—>	now saves us (not the removal of the filth of the flesh, but the answer of a good conscience toward God), through the resurrection of Jesus Christ

Is it the actual water that saves us? Absolutely not. Sins are washed away through the blood of Jesus (Matt. 26:28; Rev. 1:5). You can be dunked into water all day long, but it will mean nothing spiritually. However, when one places him/herself in the proper position for God to "operate" (cf. Col. 2:12), that person is forgiven. The act alone cannot save, but rather it "saves us … through the resurrection of Jesus Christ" (1 Pet. 3:21). We are saved by His resurrection when, and only when, we submit to baptism.

When you believe Jesus is "both Lord and Christ" (Acts 2:36; cf. John 8:24), and that He died for us and was raised from the dead (1 Cor. 15:1-4), then you must repent and confess the Lord Jesus (Rom. 10:9-10; 1 Tim. 6:12-13). Finally, you will be immersed in water for the forgiveness of sins, which are washed away by the blood of Christ. Only then are you added to His body.

Look at the answers you gave to the questions at the beginning of this chapter. Compare your answers to what the Bible teaches us regarding salvation. Have you done what the Bible commands in order to have your sins washed clean by the blood of Jesus? Think about this carefully.

When we have submitted in obedience, Jesus Christ is the source of salvation. Our "doing something" in no way changes that, because apart from His blood, we could "do something" all day long and never be saved. But God only saves us when we conform to His will.

PRESSING POINT:

You are added to the body of Jesus when doing what the Lord has said, how and why He said to do it, and after doing it, Jesus is still the source of salvation.

22

REPENTANCE

T ruly, these times of ignorance God overlooked, but now commands all men everywhere to repent, because He has appointed a day on which He will judge the world in righteousness by the Man whom He has ordained. He has given assurance of this to all by raising Him from the dead" (Acts 17:30–31).

The greatest definition of repentance in the Bible is from Matthew:

> But what do you think? A man had two sons, and he came to the first and said, "Son, go, work today in my vineyard." He answered and said, "I will not," but afterward he regretted it and went. Then he came to the second and said likewise. And he answered and said, "I go, sir," but he did not go. Which of the two did the will of his father? They said to Him, "The first." Jesus said to them, "Assuredly, I say to you that tax collectors and harlots enter the kingdom of God before you. For John came to you in the way of righteousness, and you did not believe him; but tax collectors and harlots believed him; and when you saw it, you did not afterward relent and believe him.
>
> Matt. 21:28-32

Repentance is a change of mind brought about by godly sorrow (2 Cor. 7:10) and leads to a change in life. In the parable, the first son felt sorrow over disobeying his father, and notice "he regretted it and went." The KJV uses the word "repented," while the ASV has "repented himself" and the ESV simply notes he "changed his mind." The son had a change of mind brought about by godly sorrow, which resulted in his going and working.

Repentance is vital to conversion. One cannot convert to Christ without it. Observe the application Jesus made with this parable when He was talking to "the chief priests and elders" (21:23). He likened these men to the second son, who said he would go work but did not. When Christ asked, "Which of the two did the will of his father?" the priests and elders easily knew the answer, but were in denial concerning their own lives. "The tax collectors and harlots" believed the message, which caused them to change their minds (first son), but the self-righteous Jews rejected it, while professing godliness (second son). The message should have brought about a change of mind produced by godly sorrow, but it did not. Therefore, the priests and elders did not change.

It is not enough to say you believe the gospel; you must live in accordance with it. You cannot *biblically* make the decision to be baptized if you have not committed to changing your life. For example, the Pharisees and Sadducees came to John to be baptized, but their actions clearly showed that they had not repented. Thus, John said to them: "Therefore bear fruits worthy of repentance" (Matt. 3:7, 8; Luke 3:7, 8). They had not experienced godly sorrow for their sins; therefore, baptizing them would have been in vain, just as being baptized yourself will be in vain if you have not repented.

WHAT REPENTANCE IS NOT

Repentance is not being sorry for getting caught. Paul contrasts "godly sorrow" with "the sorrow of the world" (2 Cor. 7:10). One can sorrow over having committed a sin because of the negative consequences experienced as a result of getting caught. Such sorrow, as Paul affirms, "works death."

Repentance is not godly sorrow. But wait! Godly sorrow leads to repentance, right? Yes, godly sorrow *should* bring about a change of mind (repentance), which then should lead to a change of life. Experiencing godly sorrow alone, however, is not repentance.

Repentance is not saying you are living right (lip-service). As referenced above (Matt. 21:28-32), Jesus told a parable of two sons, one said he would work in the vineyard but he did not, and the other said he would not and did. "Saying" is nothing without actually "doing." As the old adage goes, "The road to hell is paved with good intentions."

Repentance is not deciding to change only for convenience. Remember, repentance is brought about by godly sorrow; no other motivation will lead to repentance. A husband may change his mind, deciding to stop a specific sinful behavior, *only* because he is threatened by his wife and wants to maintain peace at home. God has nothing to do with this particular change of mind and, therefore, it is not true repentance.

EXAMPLES OF REPENTANCE

The Bible provides several examples of those who did and did not repent. Those who did not:

- Herod let his sensual desires get the best of him and made an oath to the daughter of Herodias to give her whatever she wanted. Her mother demanded John's head. The king was "exceedingly sorry," but "because of those who sat with him," he went through with it. His sorrow was worldly sorrow, not godly (Mark 6:22-28).

- Judas' suicide is one of the saddest accounts in all of the Bible. He realized he had sinned against Christ and tried to return the money received for betraying Christ. Tragically, this did not lead to a change of life, but rather to suicide (Matt. 27:3-5).

Those who did:

- The prodigal son "came to himself" and repented. He then went to his father, confessed his sin, and desired to make restitution (Luke 15:11-24).

- Zacchaeus "sought to see Jesus" and was pricked in his heart to do right. His repentance led to his desire to make restitution to those he harmed (Luke 19:2-10).

- Peter denied the Lord, just as He predicted (Matt. 26:34). Afterward, Peter "wept bitterly" (Matt. 26:4, 75) and experienced godly sorrow. This led him to a change of life, where after Peter stood and preached the gospel on Pentecost (Acts 2), and later suffered persecution (Acts 4, 5).

THE CHANGE OF LIFE

Notice that repentance is a change of mind that directly results in a change of life, not the changing of life itself. The Bible bears many examples illustrating this particular distinction.

On that beautiful day of Pentecost, when some 3,000 were added to the Lord's church, rebellious people who participated in the murder of Jesus Christ were converted. The change in mind led to dedicated faithfulness (Acts 2:42-47). They were converted "that day" (Acts 2:41); they did not have to make amends to everyone they had harmed through their rebellion against Christ before they were baptized. There were many who felt they could not be saved because of all the bad things they had done or thought they must make amends before they could be saved. However, notice that the Philippian jailer, who had no doubt harmed many people, in "the same hour of the night and washed their stripes. And immediately he and his family were baptized" (Acts 16:33). The jailer's change of mind led to his washing the wounds of Paul and Silas, who had been beaten and thrown into prison, as well as his being baptized into Christ for the forgiveness of sins.

Another example describes, "many of the Corinthians, hearing, believed and were baptized" (Acts 18:8). Yet among these Corinthians were "fornicators," "idolaters," "adulterers," "homosexuals," "sodomites," "thieves," the "covetous," "drunkards," "revilers," and "extortioners" (1 Cor. 6:9-11). Those who had stolen did not have pay everyone back before they could obey the gospel. The blood of Jesus Christ washed away their past sins (1 Cor. 6:11).

Your repentance will lead to a faithful life, including making amends where possible. You do not have to go on a journey "righting wrongs" before you can be baptized, but your repentance must result in the discontinuance of living in sin. As Paul wrote, "Let him who stole steal no longer, but rather let him labor, working with his hands what is good, that he may have something to give him who has need" (Eph. 4:28). The one living in sin must stop that behavior and begin to live with positive actions. Being in Christ brings the blessing of the continual cleansing of His blood, conditioned upon walking in the light (1 John 1:7-9).

If you are already a Christian, a member of the body of Christ through obedience to His gospel, then you need to confess that you have been living in sin and pray for forgiveness. After Simon was baptized (Acts 8:13), he fell back into his old ways (8:18-21), and Peter told him, "Repent therefore of this your wickedness, and pray God if perhaps the thought of your heart may be forgiven you" (8:22). Simon needed godly sorrow to produce a change of mind that would lead to a change in his behavior. He was told to pray to God. Read closely the words of John: "If we confess our sins, He is faithful and just to forgive us our sins and to cleanse us from all unrighteousness" (1 John 1:9). You must admit your "sins" and start walking "in the light" (1:7); only then will you find true repentance.

PRESSING POINT:

Repentance is a change of mind prompted by godly sorrow,
which leads to a change of life. You must repent.

23

FAITHFULLY SERVING HIM

Becoming a child of God is the beginning of a life in which one has put off the old and put on the new (Col. 3:9-10). It is a life in which one becomes a new creation in Christ (2 Cor. 5:17), walking in newness of life (Rom. 6:4). Just how is one to continue this new life?

The New Testament clearly summarizes how we might faithfully serve God. Matthew and Mark, for example, record an account of a scribe approaching Jesus (Matt. 22:34-40; Mark 12:28-34). The scribe, a Pharisee, approached Christ after "he had put the Sadducees to silence" (Matt. 12:34; see 22:23-33). He asked Jesus, "Master, which is the great commandment in the law?" (Matt. 22:36), or according to Mark 12:28, "Which is the first commandment of all?" Jesus answered,

> You shall love the Lord your God with all your heart, with all your soul, and with all your mind. This is the first and great commandment. And the second is like it: "You shall love your neighbor as yourself.
>
> Matt. 22:37-39

> The first of all the commandments is: "Hear, O Israel, the Lord our God, the Lord is one. And you shall love the Lord your God with all your heart, with all your soul, with all your mind, and with all your strength." This is the

first commandment. And the second, like it, is this: "You shall love your neighbor as yourself." There is no other commandment greater than these.

Mark 12:29-31

What Jesus affirmed in these two commandments is greatly profound, yet simple. The Master said, "On these two commandments hang all the law and the prophets" (Matt. 22:40). Mark 12:31 records, "There is none other commandment greater than these."

LOVING THE LORD

Read again Mark 12:29, which declares that there is just one God. The fact that there is only one God allows us to give all our loyalty to Him, and that is what He has asked of us. God has never accepted divided devotion. Christianity is not about doing what I am told to do just because I am told to do it. Christianity is about giving God my all. If I am not able to give my loyalty to God, then it follows that something else must have it. The scribe understood this, as he realized that the burnt offerings and sacrifices, which were offered under the Law of Moses, were no substitute for an undivided heart (Mark 12:33). Also, take note of the word "all" in Mark 12:30. The word excludes any and all division; we must devote every piece of ourselves to God and nothing else.

Mark 12:29-30 is actually a quote from Deut. 6:4-5, which is itself a collection of sermons preached by Moses to prepare people to enter the land promised them by God. Deuteronomy 6, which we encourage you to study, taught the Israelites how vital it was for them to be completely committed to serving God. Knowing this, contemplate Mark 12:30 once more: "Love the Lord thy God with all of thy heart, and with all of thy soul, and with all of thy mind, and with all of thy strength." In other words, Jesus is saying every atom of your existence ought to love God. One does not obey God out of a sense of duty or obligation; rather one obeys God because he loves Him. It is good to ask yourself from time to time questions like, "Do I seek to do God's Will because I love Him, or do I seek to do His Will for other reasons?" Love is the only acceptable answer.

LOVING OUR NEIGHBORS

You might have noticed in the above passage from Mark that Jesus mentions the second commandment under consideration. This commandment is taken from Lev. 19:18. The first commandment concerned our love for God and the other, love for mankind. Note the order: Love God, then love your neighbor. Loving your neighbor takes on a new meaning when you realize that s/he is made in the very image of God. True love for God results in true love for your neighbor, who can be anyone and everyone, as the parable of the "Good Samaritan" shows (Luke 10:30-37).

LOVING OURSELVES

Another point to consider is that there is an appropriate way to love yourself. Many problems in this world stem from the individual's lack of self-love. One way to gain respect for ourselves is to remember that God loves us. The fact that we are made in the image of God (Gen. 1:26-27) means there is a dignity that belongs to our lives. I recall hearing a man say, "God didn't make junk." God made something that He thought was worthy enough to send His Son to die for and thus save. Jesus died for something. We are to love our neighbors for the same reason we are to love ourselves: we were all made in God's image and all deemed worthy of Christ's death. Focusing upon what God has done for us can give us the proper love of self and of others that we all too easily forget.

THE GOOD SAMARITAN

On a separate occasion, Jesus was asked: "'Teacher, what shall I do to inherit eternal life?' He said to him, 'What is written in the law? What is your reading of it?' So he answered and said, 'You shall love the Lord your

God with all your heart, with all your soul, with all your strength, and with all your mind, and your neighbor as yourself.' And He said to him, 'You have answered rightly; do this and you will live'" (Luke 10:25-28).

In this one short passage, the man summed up the law, as dictated in those two commandments, and Jesus agreed with him. These lines recorded in Luke prompted one of the most beloved and well-known parables: the Good Samaritan. Within that parable, two highly respected religious men, a priest and a Levite, passed by a man who was robbed and left for dead. A Samaritan, viewed by the Jews as less than a dog, stopped and helped the man when the priest and Levite would not. It was once pointed out to me that the Bible never calls him "the Good Samaritan." People read the account and automatically recognize that he is "a good man." He loved his neighbor. The priest and Levite would have claimed to love God with everything they had, but they did not love their neighbor as themselves.

How can "all the law and the prophets" (referring to the entire Old Testament) hang "on these two commandments"? There are many more commandments, true, but if you keep these two properly, the rest will naturally follow. This is why Jesus could say, "Do this and you will live." Jesus was not dismissing the other commandments, but rather affirming that these two—love of God and love of man—are the foundation upon which all others relied. Jesus took the word love, drove a nail through it, and then said you can hang every commandment upon it. Love is the master motive.

The love we are required to share with our fellow men is not a surface-level kindness. God demands that we love deeply and truly, respecting our neighbors as fellow creations of the Lord.

> But I say to you who hear: Love your enemies, do good to those who hate you, bless those who curse you, and pray for those who spitefully use you. To him who strikes you on the one cheek, offer the other also. And from him who takes away your cloak, do not withhold your tunic either.

Give to everyone who asks of you. And from him who takes away your goods do not ask them back. And just as you want men to do to you, you also do to them likewise. But if you love those who love you, what credit is that to you? For even sinners love those who love them. And if you do good to those who do good to you, what credit is that to you? For even sinners do the same. And if you lend to those from whom you hope to receive back, what credit is that to you? For even sinners lend to sinners to receive as much back. But love your enemies, do good, and lend, hoping for nothing in return; and your reward will be great, and you will be sons of the Most High. For He is kind to the unthankful and evil. Therefore be merciful, just as your Father also is merciful.

Luke 6:27-36

This love seeks the best for others, even enemies. Jesus set a new standard for love when He taught, "A new commandment I give to you, that you love one another; as I have loved you, that you also love one another" (John 13:34). Under the old law, it was "love." However, with the gospel, it is "love as Jesus did." The commandments of loving God and our neighbors might have originated under the Old Testament, but they cross covenant lines. So it is that Paul wrote, "For the commandments, You shall not commit adultery, You shall not murder, You shall not steal, You shall not bear false witness, You shall not covet, and if there is any other commandment, are all summed up in this saying, namely, You shall love your neighbor as yourself. Love does no harm to a neighbor; therefore love is the fulfillment of the law"(Rom. 13:9-10).

To the Galatians, Paul said, "For you, brethren, have been called to liberty; only do not use liberty as an opportunity for the flesh, but through love serve one another. For all the law is fulfilled in one word, even in this: 'You shall love your neighbor as yourself.' But if you bite and devour one another, beware lest you be consumed by one another!'" (Gal. 5:13-15).

This type of love flows from the nature of God, who "shows no partiality" (Acts 10:34) and "desires all men to be saved and to come to the knowledge of the truth" (1 Tim. 2:4). We cannot love God and our neighbors properly without displaying the same love. Do you want to serve God faithfully? If so, then grasp these two commandments and hold them close to your heart, for everything else is "all summed up" in these.

PRESSING POINT:

Having a true love for God and mankind
will result in faithful service to the Lord.

APPENDIX A

TWELVE STEPS: TRUTH VS. TRADITION

We are interested in truth, which is absolute and objective, meaning it is true regardless of anything else. It stands strong despite opposition to it. It is our duty as people created in God's image to follow the evidence where it leads and accept truth, even if it flies in the face of popular belief. Jesus explained truth to some Jews, who completely rejected it, and even though they wanted to stone Jesus for proclaiming it, it remained true none-the-less (John 8:32-59). If anything contradicts biblical teaching, it should be rejected. When we speak against a particular teaching, it is not to be condescending, arrogant, or rude, but because of our love for the truth and a desire for people to obey it and go to heaven.

Alcoholism was declared a disease by the American Medical Association in 1956, which has since resulted in a widespread acceptance as truth. The movement of Alcoholics Anonymous (AA), which began in the 1930s, contributed toward it being declared as such. AA teaches the Twelve Steps in order to treat the "disease" of alcoholism, and the model has been adopted by several other addiction recovery groups since (Narcotics Anonymous, Gamblers Anonymous, Nicotine Anonymous, Cocaine Anonymous, etc.). If the disease model is flawed, however, then the Twelve Steps used to treat the "disease" are also flawed. It is important to say that the Twelve Steps contain biblical principles, and the model is a tremendous help in the recovery process. However, there are some serious flaws regarding biblical teaching, which will be addressed here in order to improve the road to recovery from addiction.

Please remember, dear reader, this is out of a love for the truth and a desire for people to obey it and go to heaven. This is not done to belittle or insult any members of Twelve Step groups (there are many such people very near and dear to my heart). There are kind and sincere people participating in these groups, whom I have the utmost respect for and a sincere hope that their battles against addiction end in victory. What will be covered in this section is not intended to attack anyone personally. We are solely concerned with how the teaching of the disease model and Twelve Step model of addiction recovery align with biblical teaching. We ask that you enter into this section with an open mind, an open Bible, and a rock solid respect for absolute truth. This model brings God into the picture, and therefore must be compared with God's inspired Word, the Bible. So we now ask that you honestly examine the evidence, despite any preconceived beliefs you have about the matter.

SPIRITUAL, BUT NOT RELIGIOUS

I recall hearing a gentleman in an AA meeting affirm that he did not need a church, as he had everything he needed in AA. This is a fairly common misconception. The Twelve Step model claims to be "spiritual, but not religious," a mindset that promotes the above problem. Study the following excerpt from an AA newsletter:

> One of the most common misconceptions about Alcoholics Anonymous is that it is a religious organization. New and prospective members in particular, when confronted with AA's emphasis on recovery from alcoholism by spiritual means, often translate "spiritual"

as "religious" and shy away from meetings, avoiding what
they perceive as a new and frightening set of beliefs.[1]

AA is making a strong attempt to distance themselves from organized
religion, so as to avoid being labeled as such. They suggest (beginning with
step 2) that one should include a higher power in the recovery process, of
which we wholly agree. However, what they fail to realize is that offering
truth claims and giving any spiritual advice at all makes them accountable
to God concerning the validity of those claims. The inspired pen wrote,
"If anyone speaks, let him speak as the oracles of God. If anyone ministers,
let him do it as with the ability which God supplies, that in all things God
may be glorified through Jesus Christ, to whom belong the glory and the
dominion forever and ever" (1 Pet. 4:11).

We are to "speak" (teach) as God has revealed unto us, and His
revelation to us is His Word, the Bible. When AA speaks of God, they
make themselves accountable to God for what they teach, and claiming to
be "not religious" does not change that responsibility in the slightest. You
cannot separate God from His Word, the Bible. Regardless of the nobility
of our cause or the sincerity of our motives, God will hold us accountable
for all we do or teach in connection with His name (Col. 3:17; Jas. 3:1).

Since His Word is the absolute standard, then it should define
"spiritual" and "religious." Does God's Word teach that one can be
"spiritual" without being "religious?" Paul uses the word "spiritual" in
connection with God's revelation of the Gospel (1 Cor. 2:6-16); it is
spiritual because it is derived from God. The man who lives according
to that revelation is, therefore, spiritual (1 Cor. 2:15-16), and contrasted
with he who does not and is foolish (1 Cor. 2:14). Peter uses the word
"spiritual" to describe the "house" built by Christ (Christians collectively)
and the worship offered by Christians to God (1 Pet. 2:4-12). Consider
also that Paul describes the person who is to restore one "overtaken in

---

1. Alcoholics Anonymous, "We Tread Innumerable Paths: Spirituality in A.A.," *A Newsletter for Professionals* (Winter 2008).

a fault" as being "spiritual" (Gal. 6:1-2). Moreover, the Galatian letter is addressed to "the churches of Galatia" (Gal. 1:2) and, thus, the "spiritual" person is a member of a local church! Furthermore, when the apostle urges that they be "restored," he indicates they have been severed from the body (organized religion) and thus are not spiritual. Therefore, the notion that one can be "spiritual" and pleasing to God, while not being involved in "organized religion," is not biblical.

There seems to be a popular mindset that "religion" is a dirty word, and that Jesus actually "hated religion." All of this was said in a poem that went viral on YouTube years ago. There are many things voiced in that particular video with which we agree, but to say Jesus hates religion is absolutely false. One person asked, "But weren't the Pharisees condemned for being religious?" Such a view stems from a misunderstanding of what it means to be religious. Jesus did heavily rebuke the Pharisees, but it was for being hypocritical, not religious. This is seen clearly in Jesus' rebuke of them in Matt. 6. Jesus addresses those who gave alms, prayed, and fasted for the sake of other men, with the intent of impressing others with their self-sacrifice. In addressing each act, Jesus refers to them as "hypocrites" (Matt. 6:2, 5, 16) because their actions were not altruistic. In His scathing rebuke, as recorded in Matthew 23, Jesus referred to them as "hypocrites" seven times (Matt. 23:13, 14, 15, 23, 25, 27, 29). They were claiming to be faithful followers of God, when in reality their hearts were corrupt before God.

The thought that Jesus was condemning religion when condemning the Pharisees is inaccurate. They were emphasizing the physical acts while neglecting the heart, and such is hypocrisy. Doing those acts is necessary, but without a pure heart, they are vain. "Checklist" religion is not the religion of the Bible; "heart" religion is. Being religious is not simply "going through the motions," which has never been, nor will ever be, pleasing to God (cf. Isa. 1:10-15). Yes, being religious involves helping the poor and needy (James 1:26-27), but it also involves keeping the commandments of Christ (1 John 2:1-6; 5:1-5). It is wrong to go through religious motions without loving your neighbor with a sincere heart, just as it is also wrong to help the needy while neglecting to serve Christ through a local church and keep His commandments.

The Bible teaches that one must be in the body of Christ in order to be saved (discussed in chapters 20-21 above). The Bible describes those within that body serving Jesus through local churches. This is the biblical pattern. We understand that the current religious scene is discouraging and may be a motivation for some to distance themselves from organized religion. The fact that many are on the wrong path, however, does not excuse us from being on the right one (Matt. 7:13-14). The answer is not to reject, but to restore, New Testament Christianity, for in the end, we will answer according to what we have done (2 Cor. 5:10; John 12:48).

It is an interesting side note that state drug treatment centers use the Twelve Step model, which requires talking about God. However, because of an apparent misapplication of separation of church and state, counselors are not supposed to teach the Bible, as the program is not to be "religious." People are expected to teach others how to recover through "spiritual" means, which incorporates God, but without enforcing His law (the Bible). Do you see the difficulty in which the counselors are bound? One cannot correctly teach another person about God without His written revelation to man. Apart from the Bible, we would not know the mind of God and could not reveal it to anyone. One has to put aside God's Word to conclude that one can be "spiritual" and pleasing to God, while not being active in the religion of Jesus Christ. The book of AA, although it does have some helpful information, cannot get a person to heaven. Only the Bible can.

A DISEASE

In 1956, The American Medical Association declared "alcoholism an illness." J. B. Myers, in his book, *Faith and Addiction*, wrote, "the disease model became the prevailing view, and in time, the sickness label spread to the abuse of other drugs and then to all kinds of problematic behaviors."[2] This mindset has "opened the floodgates," as people who exhibit unhealthy, compulsive behaviors regarding sex, gambling, eating, etc., are also said to have a disease.

Several years ago, a judge said of an admitted child rapist, "He's got a disease, just like I've got a disease," referring to his own "disease" of alcoholism. The judge compared himself, who had a drinking problem, to an admitted child rapist, on the basis of the "disease" concept.[3] The "disease" classification has led to dangerous conclusions. I used to believe that alcoholism was a "disease," and I even taught it to individuals within a treatment facility and to their families. I attempted to reconcile the disease model and the Bible for quite some time, but I eventually realized it cannot be done.

The Mayo Clinic website defines alcoholism as, "A chronic and often progressive disease that includes problems controlling your drinking, being preoccupied with alcohol, continuing to use alcohol even when it causes problems, having to drink more to get the same effect (physical dependence), or having withdrawal symptoms when you rapidly decrease or stop drinking."

Myers, in commenting on a similar definition of alcoholism, stated, "Notice that the characterization of this disease is not described in terms of biology but behavior."[4] He is absolutely correct. The characteristics of alcoholism do not fit the disease concept. I was diagnosed with ulcerative colitis in 2009 as a result of a colonoscopy. The condition of my colon, not my behavior, revealed that I indeed had the disease of ulcerative colitis. Alcoholism, however, is diagnosed through observation of one's behavior. Mayo Clinic describes the progression of "problem drinking" to "binge drinking" to "alcoholism." Alcoholism, therefore, is an addiction to alcohol, yet it is labeled as a disease. Logically, then, addiction to

---

2. J. B. Myers, *Faith and Addiction* (Lexington, KY: 2007), 54.

3. Bill O'Reilly, "What Can We Do About Ohio's Judge Connor?" *Fox News.* http://www.foxnews.com/story/0,2933,187954,00.html.

4. Myers, *Faith and Addiction*, 63.

any problematic behavior could be called a disease. As discussed in the beginning of this section, that is precisely what has happened, and negative consequences have followed.

Myers wrote, "Drinking alcohol is a behavior and not the disease it may cause. Diet and lifestyle choices can make us more susceptible to disease, but diet and lifestyle are choices, while diabetes and cancer are diseases. ... Behavior, however, is not biology, and the key to clarifying the whole issue is to separate the two. To illustrate, drinking alcohol and smoking cigarettes are behaviors, cirrhosis of the liver and lung cancer are diseases."[5]

Similarly, Dr. David J. Hanson wrote, "Smoking is not a disease but the lung cancer that it can cause is a disease. Similarly, drinking too much isn't a disease although it can cause diseases such as high blood pressure, liver cirrhosis, and fetal alcohol syndrome."[6] Drinking too much is not a disease, but rather the sign by which one is "diagnosed with the disease." It is purely behavioral.

Dr. Gabor Mate is a Canadian physician who specializes in the study and treatment of addiction. He practices in Vancouver's Downtown Eastside where many of his patients suffer from mental illness, drug addiction, HIV, or all three. He has authored four books exploring topics including attention deficit disorder, stress, developmental psychology, and addiction. In an interview regarding Mate's book, *In the Realm of Hungry Ghosts: Close Encounters with Addiction*, he was asked about his thoughts on an addiction gene. He replied,

> There is simply no science behind it, or at least the science behind it is laughably illogical and the assumptions that it is based on is that genes determine things, but first of all nobody has ever identified a specific addiction

5. Ibid., 57.

6. The Saint Jude Retreats, "The Disease Theory of Alcoholism," http://www. soberforever.net/disease-theory-alcoholism.cfm.

gene for anything. Although there may be some genetic predispositions for certain traits that may lead to addiction, for the most part genes are turned on and off by the environment.[7]

He goes on to say that these environmental factors begin "in the womb." For example, a child that is born with a crack addiction has the addiction because of its drug-induced environment in the womb, not because of an addiction gene inherited from its mother. Similarly, the idea that "an alcoholic" has no control over alcohol consumption once ingested is a dangerous concept, as Myers explains: "The danger is that people who believe they cannot control their behavior continue to behave in keeping with the sickness label assigned to them by treatment professionals, family, and friends. As a result, the disease model establishes an addiction identity that makes it difficult for change to occur."[8]

People are told that, despite being "alcohol free," they will always be alcoholics. Wayne Jackson wrote regarding this mindset,

> The notion that once one has become an "alcoholic," he will always be an alcoholic, is ludicrous. One may be "dry" for years, but, according to AA ideology, he must continually chastise himself with the mantra: "I am a recovering alcoholic." Contrast that with 1 Corinthians 6:10-11, where Paul observed that some of the Corinthian saints, at a point in their past, had been drunkards. The apostle does not endorse the notion that a former drunkard must continue to cling to that appellation for some sort of supposed psychological advantage.[9]

---

7. Interview conducted by Allan Gregg. Gregg is a Canadian pollster, political advisor, and pundit. See the interview at http://www.youtube.com/watch?v=oZ-FAX4Pz8I

8. Ibid.

9. Wayne Jackson, "What About Alcoholics Anonymous?" *Christian Courier*, https://www.christiancourier.com/articles/385-what-about-alcoholics-anonymous.

Someone might respond to this statement, "But we are not endorsing someone calling himself a drunkard for life, but rather that one realize he has the disease of alcoholism for life." We reply that this "disease" is diagnosed through the behavior of a drunkard. Why wear the label of an "alcoholic" or "alcoholism" when one no longer partakes in the activities that caused the person to receive the label in the first place? This is a negative concept and is foreign to the Scriptures.

Addiction to alcohol is a sin problem (e.g. Eph. 5:18-22; Gal. 5:19-21), as are other harmful addictions (1 Cor. 6:9-11). Dr. James Bales wrote: "Although there may be some physiological reasons why alcohol affects some more than others, alcoholism is not a disease which they have contracted because they came into involuntary contact with a germ which invaded their body. They exercised the freedom to drink, and regardless of how they may need help, they are responsible for their having become alcoholics."[10]

The only way to receive forgiveness of this sin problem is to repent and convert to Christ, becoming a new creature (1 Cor. 6:9-11; 2 Cor. 5:17).

GOD AS YOU UNDERSTAND HIM

Step three of the twelve steps model states, "Made a decision to turn our will and our lives over to the care of God as we understood Him." Notice the phrase "as we understood Him." This makes following God subjective and according to one's feelings, which actually defies God's nature. Furthermore, notice the following prayer found within the pages of the AA book:

> God, I offer myself to Thee–to build with me and to do
> with me as Thou wilt. Relieve me of the bondage of self,
> that I may better do Thy will. Take away my difficulties,
> that victory over them may bear witness to those I would

10. James Bales, "Psychiatry and Christianity" in *The Bible and Mental Health* (Stockton, CA: Courier Publications, 1998), 139.

help of Thy Power, Thy Love, and Thy Way of life. May I
do Thy will always![11]

This prayer acknowledges "Thy Way" and "Thy will," which implies
one way and one will. However, the "as we understood Him" clause
clearly conflicts with a single will and way. If God has "one way" and "one
will," then we cannot view God "as we understand Him," because our
understanding could conflict with His will. The Bible lays out a specific
path to be followed, a narrow way, as Jesus taught, "Enter by the narrow
gate; for wide is the gate and broad is the way that leads to destruction, and
there are many who go in by it. Because narrow is the gate and difficult is
the way which leads to life, and there are few who find it" (Matt. 7:13-14).

As noted earlier, one has to set aside God's Word to reach such a
conclusion. The same AA newsletter, referenced earlier, quoted Bill W.,
the organization's co-founder, as saying, "We have no desire to convince
anyone that there is only one way by which faith can be acquired. All of us,
whatever our race, creed, or color, are the children of a living Creator, with
whom we may form a relationship upon simple and understandable terms
as soon as we are willing and honest enough to try. ... We think it no
concern of ours what religious bodies our members associate themselves
with as individuals. This should be an entirely personal affair which each
one decides for himself in the light of past associations or his present
choice."[12]

He said he had "no desire to convince anyone that there is only one
way by which faith can be acquired." First, followers of God are supposed
to be concerned with convincing others to follow the proper way (Mark
16:15-16; 2 Tim. 2:2; 2 Cor. 5:11; Acts 26:28-29). Second, the Bible
affirms that there is, in fact, one way by which faith can be acquired: "So
then faith comes by hearing, and hearing by the word of God" (Rom.
10:17). One cannot manifest faith pleasing to God apart from the Bible.

---

11. Alcoholics Anonymous, 63.

12. Alcoholics Anonymous, "We Tread Innumerable Paths."

The co-founder also stated: "We think it no concern of ours what religious bodies our members associate themselves." Again, we are meant to be concerned with others' religious affiliations, for there is only one church in the eyes of Christ. The foundation for unity, as espoused in the referenced newsletter, is not religious diversity, but rather religious singularity.

CONCLUSION

The Twelve Step model has many admirable characteristics, which we have implemented in this book. They are admirable, however, because they are derived from God's Word. Is it any surprise that in searching for how to help individuals with addiction problems, they turned to biblical principles? The Bible is the answer, and in realizing such, you need to devote yourself wholly to its teachings, even when it conflicts with popularly accepted belief. Once you bring God into the picture, you have also brought in the religion of Jesus Christ. Having God without the Bible is, quite simply, not an option.

APPENDIX B

NEW CREATURE:
A TESTIMONIAL

T herefore if any man be in Christ, he is a new creature: old things
are passed away; behold, all things are become new" (2 Cor. 5:17).
What follows is a story of how a New Testament Christian overcame the
slavery of addiction through Christ. We offer this as an example of the
power of faith and strength provided to us through Christ.

"There and Back Again": An Addict's Tale
by Bruce P. Hatcher

I distinctly remember that I was in the third grade when First
Lady Nancy Reagan was promoting the "war on drugs." Programs were
popping up everywhere like "Just Say No" and "D.A.R.E." McGruff the
crime dog became an anti-drug mascot and television commercials rang
out memorable quotes like, "Son, where did you learn to use this stuff?"
"I learned it by watching you, dad!" You would have to have been living
under a rock to miss the awareness campaigns. A police officer came to
my third grade class and showed us a display box with samples of drugs
and paraphernalia. He described the effects of drugs and gave testimonies
of drug-related arrests.

I heard, believed, was afraid, and made a resolution in my mind
to never do drugs, but I was only in third grade. What did I know of

hormonal changes, peer pressure, and the rebellious tendencies that come with adolescence? Those years took me by storm. It was like one day the future was so bright that the sky was the limit; I could do anything I made up my mind to do. My mind was sharp; my body was fit. A few short years later and I was holding a gun to my head, wondering what there was worth living for? Like many other unfortunate souls in that mental state, I decided there was nothing left for me, but as I held a gun to my head, I could not pull the trigger. It wasn't the thoughts of my lifeless body being found by my family that stopped me; it wasn't any hope for the future; it was one thought. One fear.

I do not want to go to hell.

The importance of that struggle and that decision cannot be overemphasized. Two questions I hope will be helpful to you, dear reader, and allow the wasted years in my life, in some small way, to be profitable: How did I reach rock-bottom? And how did I regain hope and life again?

How Did I Hit Rock Bottom?

People use drugs for a number of reasons: to relax, to feel less shy or timid, to feel more energetic or outgoing, to cope with problems, to fit in with the crowd. These could all be summed up as self-medication for undesired symptoms and circumstances brought about by life. Then there are the people who use drugs because they are curious. Still others use them simply to feel pleasure.

Looking back, it is hard for me to point to any one reason why I used. I certainly had problems to cope with. I wanted to fit in with the crowd; I did feel less timid and more like the life of the party when drinking or drugging, so self-medication was definitely a reason. However, some of those things the police officer told us in third grade did make me curious (he described hallucinations as "hearing colors and seeing sound," an experience I never had, by the way). Finally, who doesn't like a bit of pleasure, right?

For me, it was a gradual fall. I started smoking cigarettes, which began to change the way others looked at me. I was avoided by those who didn't approve, which was great, I thought. I attracted those who were like me, which was great too. Drinking was added to our recreation list soon after, as it seemed a safe thing to do on special occasions (such as every Friday and Saturday night). After all, it was legal and adults used it, so how much trouble could it be? Occasionally, we found a "cool adult" who would buy it for us. Those adults felt just as comfortable sharing their illegal activities with us as we did. I truly tried to refuse drugs, but one adult kept persisting: "I know you must have smoked pot before; you smoke cigarettes and drink. It's no different, really." After repeatedly answering, "No!" (as I was taught in the third grade), I gave in under the intense pressure and my momentary intoxication. After that incident, I decided I loved smoking pot; I loved laughing at everything and the first-hand experience I now had brought me to the conclusion that the officer who visited my third grade class, and all adults that have never tried it, were completely wrong about drugs.

I was soon using marijuana on an almost-daily basis. I started selling anything I could find around the house (whether it was mine, my siblings, or my parents) in order to secretly purchase a sack of weed every week. I started trying to find as much time away from parental supervision as possible so that I could get high, drink, smoke, and attend parties. This included skipping school, lying about my whereabouts, and sneaking out during the night. At this point, I had a reputation as a bad kid, and I liked it.

I was absolutely fearless concerning trying other drugs. I was naive, ignorant, and arrogant enough that I thought I was in 100% control of my life. I knew more than others with more life experience, and I had more willpower than those who had succumbed to addiction. In my mind, I thought addiction was the desire I felt to keep smoking pot all the time. That's why I was fearless. So I sought out other drugs and liked to boast about all the different ones I had tried. Needless to say, my beliefs about drug addiction couldn't have been farther from the truth.

I was at a party one night, it was about 3 a.m., and everyone had left except the homeowners and myself. Most likely, they were waiting for folks to clear out and got tired of waiting for me to leave, so they decided to turn me on to something new. An eight-ball of crack-cocaine was something new for me that night, but from then on it became my constant companion in misery. I can't remember how long it took for three people to smoke it up, but I do remember that as soon as it was gone, we were all brainstorming on how to get more. That night, we spent all the cash we had, and one buddy traded the gun his father gave him. The next night I was at that house again with $40 wanting more. This was my life for the next four years. I spent my entire paycheck ($500-$700 a week), minus a tank of gas and a carton of smokes. My addiction soon had me living with drug-dealers and peddling their products for them just to maintain my habit. After I began using more product than I could pay for or replace by dealing, I had to find another place to live. My grandmother unwittingly became my enabler, allowing me to live with her rent-free, rather than suffer not knowing where I would be sleeping at night.

To this day, the most miserable feelings I have ever experienced are the withdrawals that follow quitting crack-cocaine. I would crawl-around on the floor, searching the carpet for some crumb I might have dropped, refusing to accept I had run out. I would exhaust every resource I had to get more money or something trade-worthy for another hit. Finally, I had to face the withdrawals. I would lay in bed under an electric blanket, sweating, shaking, mind-racing, and unable to sleep. Like a bad dream that keeps waking you up all night long and leaves you exhausted, all I could do was suffer, lie awake, and think of all the bad things I had done, all the people I had wronged, the shame I was causing my family, and the worthlessness of my existence. I then knew what addiction was, and I knew I was powerless. I wanted it all to be over but had no clue how it would ever happen. I wanted to die. It was there in my grandmother's house that I picked up the pistol she had bought to protect herself when home alone and, crying, I put it to my head.

How Did I Find Happiness Again?

I said that my reaching rock bottom was gradual, and so was my recovery. I agree with popular sentiments, "Admitting you have a problem is the first step to recovery." It wasn't very difficult for anyone, including myself, to see that I had a problem, a problem that seemed so much bigger than myself, bigger than I could possibly deal with alone. I was so physically addicted that when I got my hands on any money, I would think of the drug and immediately get a nauseating feeling, vomit, and begin shaking. There's no presence of will-power, hope, dignity, or the like when "geeking" (slang-term for crack-use behavior and withdrawal symptoms). All the attributes, mindsets, and abilities needed to overcome addiction are counteracted by the addiction itself. It would be like trying to pick-up a box while you are sitting inside it—impossible! Therefore, the second most important thing to my recovery was finding someone outside that box to help me lift it. That help knocked on the door one day.

My father showed up at my grandmother's house one day, visibly disturbed. His voice quivered, and I could see his pain as he said, "The family has met and discussed your drug addiction. We love you, and because we do, we can't watch you do this to yourself any longer. Until you begin making an effort to get help, we don't want to see you anymore; not on Thanksgiving, not at Christmas, not at all."

I know many popular talk-show hosts would rake my father across the coals for not supporting his son unconditionally. To them, it would seem like a lack of love, a move of cowardice. But what my father did was give "tough-love," the deepest, hardest love to give, and the love I needed most. Within two weeks, I could not bear the torment any longer. I called my father and said, "I have an appointment to enter rehabilitation. Will you drive me there?" He helped me bear that burden. Dad, I love you!

My recovery was still gradual. I made good progress in rehabilitation, I learned what was happening physically in my brain when I used. I met others struggling to rebuild their lives like myself. One sponsor shared a thought with me that I can't help but remember. He asked if I had ever crawled on my hands and knees looking for crumbs while drugging. Of course I answered that I had, to which he replied, "If you were willing to get on your knees for the drug, why not get on your knees when you pray tonight?" I did, and I still find it soothing and appropriate when my heart is heavy.

Rehab definitely pointed me towards recovery, but I failed to follow through with some of the keys to success like, "change playgrounds and playmates." About a month out of rehab, I was back to using. Another year or so went by before I was finally arrested in front of a crack house that the police were monitoring. I was taken downtown where I spent two-weeks, at which point I was moved to a federal penitentiary for another ten weeks. I consider jail to have been a blessing at that point in my life, a time that was very important to my recovery.

I observed a contrast in the attitudes of the inmates. Some talked of changing their lives, while others only talked about getting out and returning to their old ways, as if jail was just some minor inconvenience along the way. I saw men being released, but before my release date came, they were back for repeating the same crime. I saw men in their fifties and sixties in jail for drug use. These things caused me to remember how I always thought this was a phase. I'm just having fun for a while; later, I'll change. No one ever says, "I'm gonna be a drug addict when I grow up." Nobody plans to have that life. Yet here I was, participating in a very live-case study. I reasoned, "I have been clean longer than I can remember being clean since I was fourteen. If I don't stop, I'll be like those old men over there. If my attitude doesn't change now, I'll be a repeat offender like those guys and have a calloused attitude, and I will never change. This is the best chance I may ever have to change!"

There was a man in prison there, I don't remember much about him except everyone called him Brother Roscoe and that he was on an almost disgusting religious-kick; "Jesus-this" and "Jesus-that," he would say; "hallelujahs" and "amens" by the truckload. I had grown up in a Christian family and was baptized at nineteen, even while struggling to overcome drugs. But because I could not overcome my addiction, I quickly lost hope, felt ashamed, and quit attending. I did not think Jesus was the answer to my problem, and I didn't want to humiliate myself again by jumping on the Jesus bandwagon to look like this fool Brother Roscoe.

One day, Brother Roscoe made another attempt to reach me by asking me to come to religious services. The thought of getting out of that pod (a large cell with about 50 inmates inside) was alluring, and Brother Roscoe's happiness and hopefulness made me curious, so I heard myself say, "Yes, I'll come." I was given a Bible at that meeting, a sermon was preached, men shared their regrets and fears, prayers were offered, songs were sung, and I went back to my pod feeling a lot better. I decided I'm not going to be a hypocrite; I'm going to be real about this, "true to the game," as I said it then.

I began reading my Bible. There were not many distractions, so I read a lot. In fact, by the time I was released a month later, I had read from Matthew through Revelation, and had started the Old Testament, reading as far as 2 Samuel. I began to have religious discussions with other religious-minded inmates, sometimes throughout the night while the rest of the pod slept. I began to find answers to religious questions that for a long time had puzzled me, leading to other questions. My lack of answers had become a major source of spiritual discouragement. I began to have a hunger for God's Word, so I asked a trustee to bring me religious material from the library. He would bring me a book or two. Then, when I was finished with them, I would give it back so he could bring me more.

One day, I got jumped by an inmate who, it seems, just wanted to make himself look tough by picking on someone smaller. I had to be taken to the doctor for stitches in my left eyebrow. Because I would not tell the officers who did it to me (telling-on someone in jail can be suicidal), I was placed in solitary confinement for the two weeks leading up to my release. Little did they know how much I appreciated it, as I had more quiet time to read, study, and pray. There I prayed a prayer I will never forget, "God, every time in the past that I have prayed, I have done so asking for your help. This time I ask no favors. I deserve my punishment. But I promise you this: When I get out of here, I will dedicate the rest of my life to you; I will attend church, I will help others, and if I should ever have a family, I will teach them to do the same." My son was born about ten years later; I named him Nathan, which means "a gift from God." That name reminds me of my promise to God, but I have found I cannot out-give Him.

After my release, I began attending a church that resembled the church I read about in the Bible, the church that is named in the Bible, the church of Christ (Rom. 16:16). I asked the preacher soon after, "What should I do to stay clean? The statistics are against me, and I'm so scared of going back." The preacher, Ed Ballard, said to me, "Get involved with the church, be here every time the doors are open, take part in every activity, take part in service in the public assembly, study, and pray." My dear reader, I cannot give you any better advice today. It has served me well; I have grown in knowledge and ability; I have never looked back and said, "Those were happier times back then." Each day, I grow closer to God and to my reward.

What contributed to my recovery? First, I realized I had a problem. Second, I had someone who cared enough about me to give "tough-love." Third, I had time to seriously consider and meditate about where my decisions were taking me. Fourth, I had some divine intervention, not in a miraculous way, but by simply reading God's soul-saving message and meditating on it. Fifth, I effectively used the tools God has given to all men to aid in their conversion—I obeyed God's plan of salvation. Now I walk in newness of life, pressing forward every day.

Final Thoughts

I attended AA, CA, and NA meetings for some time after my rehabilitation. It was therapeutic to a degree. I have friends who are in recovery and have attended them for years that feel as though those meetings are all that keep them from using. I mean no disrespect to those who are striving to live clean and sober lives in any way they can. But, my friends, I would ask everyone to consider the following:

> Grace and peace be multiplied unto you through the knowledge of God, and of Jesus our Lord, According as his divine power hath given unto us all things that pertain unto life and godliness, through the knowledge of him that hath called us to glory and virtue: Whereby are given unto us exceeding great and precious promises: that by these ye might be partakers of the divine nature, having escaped the corruption that is in the world through lust.
>
> 2 Peter 1:2-4

I would ask you, my dear friend, if sobriety could be considered as part of what "pertains to life and godliness?" I think you would agree that it does and, if so, then God has "given unto us all things pertaining" to it—please read carefully—"through the knowledge of Him," and with that comes exceedingly great promises. I believe all the support one needs to get clean and sober is available through His plan, and that includes His church.

If you are going to attend meetings for the rest of your life, why not attend meetings of the church where both the body and soul may profit? If you are going to read a book (like AA's blue book), why not read the black book, the Bible, that is profitable to you not only in this life but in the next as well? If you are going to stand up before men and confess like I did, "My name is Bruce. I am an addict," then why not stand and say, "I believe that Jesus Christ is the Son of God" and save your soul, as well as your body? I urge you to be a recipient of the peace that passes all understanding, which Jesus Christ made possible. He came that you might have life and that you might have it more abundantly (John 10:10).

I have attended the funerals of old friends who never escaped the clutches of substance abuse, young men who, like myself, were born into Christian families. Why was I afforded this opportunity when they were not? The only conclusion I can come up with is this: the life I was living was also close to ending on a much sadder note. Every moment on this earth is an opportunity to observe where our life is headed without God and prepare for eternity. Waiting for you is another life in Christ, where God has a plan and purpose for you. If your old life is already shattered, then you have nothing left to lose.

CONCLUSION

There is a saying in recovery circles, which I quite like: "One day at a time." The saying is an echo of the words of Jesus, as recorded in Matthew 6:34: "Therefore do not worry about tomorrow, for tomorrow will worry about its own things. Sufficient for the day is its own trouble." These words connect with Jesus' previous lessons regarding the folly of worry and the necessity of depending upon and trusting in God. Jesus declared: "But seek first the kingdom of God and His righteousness, and all these things shall be added to you" (Matt. 6:33).

Seek to do God's will as revealed by His Word, focusing upon serving Him to the best of your ability *today*. This is not to say do not plan ahead (as a reading of this book shows), but rather do not let worries of the future hinder you from accomplishing what you should now for the Lord. Regardless of what happens in the future, you can Press Forward today. The most important question, however, is will you?

ACKNOWLEDGMENTS

This book would not be possible without the help of Torrey Clark, Charles Harris, and Bruce Hatcher. Week after week after week, they helped me with this project. It absolutely would not be what it is without them. In fact, I believe it would not be at all. I am grateful to Dan Cates, Jennifer Hatcher, and Mary Beth Kinchen for proofreading, and to Jena Webb for editing. I am grateful to Bruce Hatcher for submitting his story of overcoming addiction. I am grateful to Jerry Martin, Michael Shank, and Dan Cates for writing commendations for the book. Finally, thanks to Start2Finish for publishing this book.

Trent Childers

CPSIA information can be obtained at www.ICGtesting.com
Printed in the USA
LVOW05s1239020115

421073LV00004B/6/P